The Story of
WORLD
WAR I

by ROBERT LECKIE

Adapted for young readers from
The American Heritage History of
WORLD WAR I
by the Editors of AMERICAN HERITAGE
with narrative by S. L. A. Marshall
Brigadier General, USAR (ret.)

RANDOM HOUSE NEW YORK

The Editors wish to thank Anthea Lingeman, who designed this adaptation, and Joseph L. Gardner, Managing Editor of *The American Heritage History of World War I*, who assisted in the preparation of text and captions. Grateful acknowledgment is made to F. B. Rockwell, copyright owner of the song sheet cover illustration on page 86; the title "Over There" and first two lines (page 111) of the song by George M. Cohan (© copyright 1917, renewed 1945, Leo Feist, Inc., New York, N.Y.) are used by permission; the lines from Rupert Brooke's *The Soldier* on page 41 are reprinted by permission of Dodd, Mead and Company, Inc., New York, from the *Collected Poems of Rupert Brooke*, copyright 1915 by Dodd, Mead and Company, copyright 1943 by Edward Marsh.

Front cover: Canadian troops go over the top at Vimy Ridge (Imperial War Museum, London). Title Page: American troops trudge through the rain (Print Division, New York Public Library). Chronology: French drummer by Ricardo Flores (Musée de la Guerre, Paris). End sheets: British troops advance across barbed wire at the Somme (Imperial War Museum, London). Below: German prisoners and Allied stretcher bearers cross a Flanders battlefield (Department of National Defence, Ottawa, Canada).

Table of Contents

Archduke Francis Ferdinand, wearing a plumed dress helmet (extreme right), and his wife Sophie were photographed at the beginning of their state visit to Sarajevo. As their open car made its way through the crowded streets a young man stepped forward and fired two pistol shots at the royal couple. Gavrilo Princip was seized only minutes after the fatal shooting; in the photograph at right, taken at that moment, he is second from right. This young man, who in a way fired the first shot of World War I, was later convicted but not executed because he was only nineteen years old.

PROLOGUE

Dawn of June 28, 1914, was breaking over Sarajevo. At the Begova Mosque, a sleepy-eyed crier groped his way around a narrow spiral staircase leading to the top of the minaret. Reaching it, he stepped out onto the balcony, flung his arms wide, and began the ancient Moslem chant:

"Hear, O Faithful. There is no God but Allah!"

Slowly, the sleeping city stirred awake. The market place filled. The day grew hot. Europeans in this capital city of the Austrian province of Bosnia moved toward the parade route over which the Archduke Francis Ferdinand of Austria was to travel that day. From the little neighboring kingdom of Serbia came seven other spectators. They were young men with burning eyes who had pistols and bombs hidden on their persons. They hated the Archduke Francis Ferdinand because they believed that he stood in the way of joining Bosnia together with other Slavic states in a Greater Serbia. And therefore they had come to Sarajevo to kill him. They, too, joined the crowds thronging to the parade route. They separated, one by one, to take up stations from which they might fire bullets or hurl bombs into the car carrying the Archduke and his beloved wife, Sophie.

Francis Ferdinand and Sophie were in the second limousine of a four-car motorcade. At the Čumuria Bridge the royal car passed the first assassin, Mohammed Mehmedbašić. He froze, and the car passed on. It came abreast of the second assassin, Nedjelko Čabrinović—and he hurled his bomb at the green feathers on the Archduke's helmet.

The royal car leaped forward, the bomb passed behind Sophie's back, and the Archduke quickly flicked it onto the street—where it exploded with a roar. A flying splinter struck Sophie in the cheek, and others wounded spectators.

Alarmed now, the first two cars sped on to City Hall. They swept by three more assassins, who did nothing to stop them. More furious than frightened, the Archduke leaped out and seized the arm of the mayor of Sarajevo.

"One comes here for a visit and is received with bombs! Mr. Mayor, what do you say? It's outrageous! All right, now you may speak."

The mayor spoke soothingly, and at length the Archduke recovered his composure. Pulling himself together, Francis Ferdinand then remembered the innocent spectators wounded in the bomb blast. He would go to the hospital to see them. He told Sophie that she need not share the risk.

"No," she said firmly, "I must go with you," and the Archduke consented.

The motorcade departed, driving past the sixth assassin, who made no move. At the next intersection the first two cars made a right turn into Francis Joseph Street. "What's this?" cried a general in the Archduke's car. "We've taken the wrong way!"

The driver stopped. He prepared to turn around. Five feet away stood the seventh and boldest of the assassins: Gavrilo Princip, with gun drawn.

Twice the little pistol snapped, and one bullet struck the Archduke in the neck and the other hit Sophie in the stomach. They sat upright, gazing ahead—as though unscathed. The car roared away, and then a stream of blood spouted from the mouth of Francis Ferdinand. Sophie screamed.

"For heaven's sake, what's happened to you?" she cried, and then crumpled in her seat. The stricken Archduke looked at her and gasped: "Sophie dear, Sophie dear, don't die! Stay alive for our children!" Then he too collapsed. Someone leaned over him and asked if he was in pain. "It is nothing. It is nothing," he murmured, and those were his last words.

Sophie was dead before she could be removed from the car, and the Archduke Francis Ferdinand died soon after.

It was not quite noon in Sarajevo; and yet, the shadows of a long and dreadful night were already lengthening over all the world.

The Austrian cavalry gallops past Wilhelm II and Francis Joseph (background) in a pre-war review. The painting reflects a misconception of that era—that war was splendid.

WHY IT BEGAN 1

In so far as any single event can provoke a war, the assassination of the Archduke Francis Ferdinand started World War I. It was not the cause of that dreadful holocaust, however. It was only the spark that exploded the European powder keg.

The true cause of World War I was the tension that was rising among the rival imperial powers of Europe, and especially the enmity that existed between France and Germany.

In the year 1870, the Germans had humbled the French in a lightning campaign. They had forced them to pay an immense war bill and wrested from them the provinces of Alsace and Lorraine (see map on page 12). When the French Assembly had agreed to this humiliation in 1871, the deputies from the lost provinces had left the hall in tears.

"We proclaim forever the right of Alsatians and Lorrainers to remain members of the French nation," they secretly vowed. "We swear for ourselves, our constituents, our children and our children's children to claim that right for all time, by every means, and in the face of the usurper."

Thus, a "sacred anger" was born in the hearts of the French. They burned to avenge their shame and to recover the lost provinces. Yet, this was not possible. Germany was now allied with Austria-Hungary and Russia. Such an alliance provided an enormous pool of men and arms: it simply terrified Europe. Moreover, England, to whom France might have turned for support, was remaining aloof from involvement in European politics.

But then, in 1882, the young Kaiser Wilhelm II succeeded to the imperial German throne. He was a swaggerer and a braggart, a man who always threatened war although he did not really want to make it. He was also pious and patriotic and he certainly meant well for Germany. The rattling of the young Kaiser's saber so disturbed the Czar of Russia that he allowed himself to be pushed into an alliance with an all-too-willing France.

Thus the Double Entente was created by France and Russia. Germany and Austria continued in a Double Alliance, which became the Triple Alliance after Italy joined. A newly formed nation, Italy feared France and felt that such a move was necessary to preserve her freedom.

That was the situation as the 1800's neared their end. England still possessed the balance of power between the opposing blocs. So long as she did not join either alliance it did not seem that the peace of Europe would be disturbed. Without regard to that delicate balance, Germany began to expand her empire. Her merchant fleet grew to rival the maritime supremacy of England, and the Kaiser openly boasted of building a fighting navy equal to the British mammoth. In 1904 he publicly styled himself Admiral of the Atlantic Ocean.

England could no longer afford to ignore Germany. She was being challenged as mistress of the seas, the unique position that had allowed her to develop into the world's foremost trader. England entered upon secret discussions with France. She became semiattached to the Franco-Russian entente. Her obligation was kept secret, however, and it was also very vaguely defined.

Then, in 1905, the world was stunned by the defeat of Russia by Japan. Not only had a new power arisen in the shape of Japan, but the Russian giant was shown to be a big man with very weak legs. France and England were alarmed, Germany and Austria overjoyed. But the powers on both sides had completely misunderstood the meaning of the Russian defeat in the Far East.

It meant chiefly that Russia would now turn from her eastern frontiers in Asia and concentrate on her European borders. She would protect herself against Austria-Hungary and Germany. She would cast her eyes south, toward the Slavic races that had traditional ties to Russia but were now part of the Austro-Hungarian Empire. And she would look to-

PREWAR EUROPE

Prewar Europe was dominated by the great empires of Austria-Hungary and Germany, which together with Turkey and Bulgaria formed the Central Powers (black). Caught between these powers was Serbia, which sided with the Allies (white). The largest of the Allies was Russia, whose vast territory then included the Baltic States and Poland. Greece, Portugal, and Rumania joined the Allies in 1916 and 1917. The six neutral nations are shown in brown.

ward Turkey, which could give her an outlet to the Mediterranean. That was why Russia was pleased to see Turkey all but driven from Europe by the two Balkan wars of the early 1900's. That was why Russia assured little Serbia on the borders of Austria-Hungary that she would never desert her. That was why in 1914 an American diplomat in Europe cabled President Wilson: "Everybody's nerves are tense. It only requires a spark to set the whole thing off." And that was why the young Serbian assassin who fired his bullets into the bodies of the Archduke and his wife accidentally sent the sparks flashing into the powder keg of Europe.

"Serbia must learn to fear us again," the Austrian minister to Serbia wired home. "Otherwise, our old border regions, and not just the annexed provinces, will be in danger."

Many European monarchs were related, but the family ties did not prevent them from warring with each other. In the photograph directly above, first cousins Czar Nicholas II of Russia (left) and King George V of England (then Duke of York) are shown with similar beards and yachting outfits. Above left, Nicholas (arms folded) chats with another cousin, Germany's Wilhelm II.

The man who read that dispatch, the warlike Count Leopold von Berchtold, did not need such advice. Berchtold was the Foreign Minister of Austria, and he had already reacted to the assassination of the Archduke by proposing to invade Serbia. A lady's man, a liar, and a luxury-lover, it was this man—more than Kaiser Wilhelm himself—who was chiefly responsible for making sure that the sparks of Sarajevo produced a real explosion.

Although his plan to invade was rejected because Austria was not yet mobilized for war, Berchtold was still determined to humble the Serbs. And because he thought world opinion would accept his description of Serbia as the homeland of assassins, he believed Austria could get anything she wanted out of the little country. First he protected himself by securing the Kaiser's promise to back Austria if she were attacked by Russia; then he sent Serbia an

13

ultimatum. He gave Austria's little neighbor only forty-eight hours to reply to demands that no self-respecting nation could accept.

Sir Edward Grey, the British Foreign Minister, read a copy of the ultimatum and called it the strongest demand ever made by one state on another.

Idling aboard the royal yacht *Hohenzollern* off Norway, Kaiser Wilhelm read it and commented to his naval aide: "A spirited note, what?"

Why neither England nor Germany did not realize that the ultimatum was nothing less than an excuse to start a war has never been made clear. The Kaiser, of course, still foolishly believed Berchtold's assurance that he was not out to gobble up Serbia. In England, Sir Edward Grey did not know that the Kaiser had been duped into giving Austria a blank check against Serbia. Moreover, Sir Edward dreaded the idea of entangling his country in a European conflict, and the British Cabinet was faced with the problem of an uprising in Ireland.

But the Serbs knew what the ultimatum meant. "Well," one of them said, "there is nothing to do but die fighting." Even so, Serbia's reply to Austria was far from being warlike.

Nevertheless, Austria rejected it. On July 28, she declared war on Serbia.

Now Russia began mobilizing. On July 31, the Germans called upon her to stop. Russia refused, and Germany and Russia were at war.

Next, France ordered general mobilization. She was bound to aid her ally, Russia, and to defend herself against her old enemy, Germany.

On August 2, Italy declared herself a neutral. She claimed that Austria's actions freed her from her obligation to the Triple Alliance.

Thus, the Great Powers were arrayed against each other. France and Russia were at war with the two empires sandwiched between them: Germany and Austria-Hungary. What, the world asked breathlessly, would England do?

England, to her sorrow, had no choice. Her rulers had already secretly committed her to a military agreement with France and Russia. In addition, England could not afford to see the European coast occupied by Germany. Still, the English did no more at first than to promise France to protect her coasts against German attack.

Whether or not England entered the war on the side of her French and Russian allies depended on one crucial question: Would Germany respect the neutrality of Belgium.

The answer was "No!" and it had been given a decade ago.

In 1905, Count Alfred von Schlieffen, Chief of the German General Staff, had drawn up the famous Schlieffen Plan for war against France and Russia. Many historians have described this plan as a masterpiece created by a military mastermind. But it was not a great idea, nor the idea of a great mind. It was merely a recognition of two facts of European history and geography: one, that Russia was always slow to mobilize; two, that Belgium was the gateway to France.

The sly actions of Count Berchtold, the Austrian Prime Minister, helped fan the Serbian crisis into a European war.

In more carefree times, Emperor Francis Joseph was portrayed as an Alpine huntsman.

Schlieffen proposed to overwhelm France with his main strength while a smaller force held off slow-moving Russia, after which both armies would join to finish off the Czar. To do this Germany could not attack through the rugged terrain along the Franco-German border. That would take too long: before Paris could be reached, the Russians might be attacking Germany's eastern frontier in strength. No, the quickest way was over the Belgian lowlands opening on France's northern border. It was longer in distance—250 air miles as opposed to 180—but it was shorter in time.

The Schlieffen Plan was approved, even though Germany knew that Belgium was a neutral. That little kingdom between France and Holland had been formed in 1831, and England was one of the nations pledged to guarantee her neutrality. To violate her, however, was considered "a military necessity" by the German war lords. She would not fight, it was believed, nor would England be so foolish as to enter the war merely to fulfill a promise.

But England would. On August 3, Germany shocked the world by demanding free passage through Belgium. England, not only to honor her obligation but also to save France and destroy a menacing rival, responded to the German move by demanding that the invasion of Belgium be halted.

The German Chancellor raged: "Just for a scrap of paper, Great Britain is going to make war on a kindred race." In a way he was right. At midnight, August 4, Britain declared war on Germany.

In London that evening Sir Edward Grey stood at a window with a friend, watching as the lamps were being lit on the street below. Sir Edward's gentle bird watcher's eyes were sad as he turned to say:

"The lamps are going out all over Europe."

15

Exuberant Berliners, including a young woman and a civilian (far right) who has traded his straw hat for a helmet, join arms with their soldiers during a military parade.

FIRST BLOOD 2

Six million armed men were moving across the face of Europe during that fateful August of 1914.

According to schedule, Germany had wheeled 1,500,000 soldiers toward France and placed another 500,000 facing east against Russia. Austria confronted Serbia and Russia with 500,000 troops.

Against these foes France mustered about 1,600,000 men—to be supplemented by another 100,000 apiece from Britain and Belgium—and Russia called up 1,400,000 more.

These were the early dispositions. Britain would go far, far beyond her originally small contribution; the Russian mobilization alone would place 12,000,000 men under arms; Germany's would rise to 11,000,000; and by the time the war had spread and become truly global there would be more than 65,000,000 men mobilized.

No one, of course, even suspected that such a catastrophe was at hand. Everyone expected the war to be short, if not sweet. "You will be home before the leaves have fallen from the trees," the Kaiser told his departing soldiers. On both sides the scenes of mobilization were gay and carefree. Only Lord Kitchener, the British War Minister, and a few others seemed to understand that there was a long nightmare ahead. Almost no one realized that warfare had changed from "the sport of kings" (in which a few thousand troops maneuvered on an open field) into the mechanical butchery of millions of men massed like moles in networks of underground mud.

The French so little understood the changes in warfare caused by the Industrial Revolution that they sent their men into battle still wearing coats of horizon blue and bright red pants. These were splendid targets for German machine gunners, who were wisely dressed in field gray.

France was confident of quick victory—if only because the French had a creed of relentless attack.

It was like a religion with them. Their Commander in Chief, General Joseph Jacques Césaire Joffre, also believed in frontal assault. Joffre was an imposing man with a huge frame, a big white walrus mustache, and a great paunch. But his was not an original mind. He believed what his staff had told him, and that was that *cran* and *élan*, pluck and verve, would beat the detestable *Boche*. As a result, "Papa" Joffre proposed to hurl his divisions headlong against the Germans at roughly what he believed to be the center of their line.

And that, except for a change in the German command, would have been just what the Schlieffen Plan had ordered. General Helmuth von Moltke had succeeded Schlieffen as Chief of the General Staff. He had no great military ability, but he happened to be a favorite of the Kaiser's. He was also the nephew of the great Helmuth von Moltke, the soldier who had conquered France in the Franco-Prussian War. That was the German commander's chief claim to fame. Worse, in 1914 he was already sixty-six years old, and he had by then begun to make drastic revisions in the Schlieffen Plan.

The old proposal was to send a powerful right wing through Belgium while luring the French armies into Germany with a weak left wing. Then the right wing would come around Paris and smash into the French rear. Schlieffen's dying words were, "Keep the right wing strong." But Moltke weakened it, while strengthening the left. As a result, when the French divisions heaved forward they were not allowed to rush into difficult terrain where they would eventually be caught between two fires. They were hurled back into France.

Although the stand of the German left wing wrecked the Schlieffen Plan for good and all, General Joffre had no way of knowing this. He could not take heart from messages telling him that everywhere along the front the French armies were meeting defeat and retreating. Nor did he understand,

in those early August days, that the true threat to France was racing down through Belgium to his rear.

Albert, King of the Belgians, was tall, handsome, and a man of many interests. He was a mountain climber, a man who drove a motorcycle and piloted an airplane, and a devourer of books. King Albert was also very brave, and he did not hesitate to reject the German demand for free passage through his country, even though he knew it would be impossible for his tiny army to halt the giant invader from the east.

Still, it might upset the German timetable—especially at the fortress of Liège. Liège was the gateway to the Belgian plain. Once in control of Liège the Germans could seize the network of railroads and highways running south across level ground into northern France. To Liège King Albert sent his fiercest commander, General Gérard Leman, under orders to "hold to the end." General Leman had about twenty-five thousand men against a German spearhead of sixty thousand. On August 4, he began the defense of Liège.

The Germans opened the battle under the direction of an unknown colonel of fusiliers named Erich Ludendorff. As his men entered Belgian soil, and engaged that little kingdom in the first war in its history, Ludendorff complained that armed civilians were resisting him. They were rounded up and shot to death without trial. Next, Belgian priests were executed on the false charge that they were organizing civilian resistance. Thus, even as the war began, so did German atrocities.

German arms, meanwhile, were being stunned. The Belgian soldiers around Liège fought like tigers. Their four frontier forts poured a terrible fire into Germans trying to cross the Meuse River on pontoons. The river was reddened with blood. Even so,

the Germans were brave—and kept on coming. They were also green, and they committed such deadly errors as attempting to charge up slopes into machine gun nests. They were sickled to the ground. At the very outset of the war the machine gun was proving that the headlong, massed charge was a thing of the past.

And now the star of Erich Ludendorff began to rise above the smoking, blackened ruins of the countryside around Liège. He put a force of German cavalry on one of the routes to the rear of the Liège defenses. This shook General Leman more than was necessary. He withdrew part of his troops to guard his rear, leaving the spaces between his forts open and unguarded. At this point Ludendorff took over a brigade whose general had been killed. He led it through one of the gaps and penetrated into the city of Liège itself. The forts had not yet fallen, of course, but Germany had its first hero: the awkward problem of Belgium now seemed soluble. General Moltke could stop quaking in his boots, and the dreadful German siege artillery could start rumbling toward the front.

The world had never known anything like these German monsters. One was the famous Big Bertha, a 16.5-inch mammoth that could hurl a shell weighing eighteen hundred pounds a distance of nine miles. The nearest thing to this in those days was the British 13.5-inch naval rifle. A Belgian statesman who saw one of these 16.5-inch guns being dragged through Liège itself has written of the shock he felt upon seeing it:

"The monster advanced in two parts, pulled by thirty-six horses. The pavement trembled. The crowd remained mute with consternation at the appearance of this phenomenal apparatus . . . Hannibal's elephants could not have astonished the Romans more! The soldiers who accompanied it marched stiffly with an almost religious solemnity. It was the Belial of cannons! In the Parc d'Avroy it was carefully mounted and scrupulously aimed. Then came the frightful explosion. The crowd was flung back, the earth shook like an earthquake and all the windowpanes in the vicinity were shattered. . ."

One by one the Belgian forts crumbled under the impact of those monster shells. Of twelve of them

only Fort Loncin was still standing by August 15. General Leman was at Loncin, still determined to fight to the end. But then a shell exploded in the fort's magazine and Loncin went up with a roar. Leman's body was found under a block of masonry. "Respect the General, he is dead," a wounded Belgian adjutant told the German soldiers. But Liège's fierce defender was not dead. Surrendering his sword to the German commander, General Emmich, he said proudly: "I was taken unconscious. Be sure to put that in your dispatches."

"Military honor has not been violated by your sword," Emmich replied. "Keep it."

Nevertheless, Liège had fallen—and the road to Paris lay open.

The stand at Liège had upset the German time-table very little. Before the fortress city fell, two German armies were already rolling south. Still, the image of "brave little Belgium" had evoked the admiration of the world, while German atrocities had swung world opinion against the Central Powers. And the Allied forces preparing to receive the oncoming Germans were encouraged by the splendid fight that King Albert's soldiers had put up.

By then the B.E.F. had arrived in France. Num-

Throughout the European countryside in 1914, homeless people (below) ran before the onslaught of advancing armies. It became clear that this would be a total war in which women and children as well as soldiers would be annihilated. At left, civilians survey the rubble of Ortelsburg in East Prussia, which was destroyed by the Russians. Above is the Cloth Hall in Ypres, which was shelled by German guns in November, 1914.

Kluck   *Bülow*

bering about one hundred thousand Regulars, most of whom were deadly rifle shots, the B.E.F. was called "the contemptible little army" by the Germans. It was led by Field Marshall Sir John French. He placed it on the left of the French Fifth Army and awaited the German attack (see map on page 29).

It was coming hard as a pitchfork thrust, southwestward out of Belgium. The eastern prong, the Second Army, was under General Karl von Bülow; the west prong, the First Army, was under General Alexander von Kluck. Kluck, a gambler and a driver, could have swept out wide to his west to come around the B.E.F. in his swing around Paris. But Bülow was in charge of the two-pronged sweep. A nervous man, he ordered Kluck to stay in close.

As a result, the B.E.F. and the French Fifth Army —chiefly the B.E.F.—were able to check the onrushing Germans. British rifle fire cut them down in droves during a fight in the slate dumps, slag piles, and oat fields of the area around Mons. But the Germans pressed on, battering the British with their artillery. The French Fifth had already fallen back on Sir John's right, and now the British right flank was open. Sir John pulled back. His men turned and fought again at a place called Le Cateau. They did not appear contemptible then, and they won a victory. But their losses were frightful. One day the survivors of that brave B.E.F.—often so grossly mismanaged by Sir John—would proudly call themselves "the Old Contemptibles." But in these days of the dying August they were weary and footsore. Their fight was made more difficult by the eruption

in their midst of masses of terrified civilians fleeing the German armies.

"A grey mob, grey because the black clothes most of them wore were covered with dust, was filing endlessly by," a young Allied officer wrote. "They occupied the whole width of the road . . . [going] in absolute silence, the only sound being that of very tired feet dragging . . . Men and women with set staring faces, carrying heavy bundles . . . formed a background of grim despair."

Such tragic obstacles to military movement were to become common in the twentieth century, but then they were new. Paralyzing the retreating British and French, they served as an advance guard for the onrushing columns of Kluck and Bülow—jubilant, now, and panting for Paris.

Meanwhile, General Joffre still thought that the attack from Belgium was a minor one. Still full of *cran* and *élan*, he sent the flower of French manhood charging into the meat grinder on the German border. Some three hundred thousand Frenchmen would be lost in the romantic delusion that dash and ardor could crack fixed positions and quench the firepower of a strong enemy. At last, turning from this miserable debacle known as the Battle of the Frontiers, Joffre realized that France's true peril lay in the down-charging armies of Kluck and Bülow—and the three more that were now pouring south between Bülow's men and the border.

By then a great battle had been begun on the eastern frontier between Germany and Russia. It was to have a vital effect on the course of the war.

The battle began in the province of East Prussia, birthplace of the Prussian military spirit that organized and informed the German nation. At first the fighting went against the German army led by the panicky General Max von Prittwitz. Two Russian armies drove him back. Prittwitz ordered a retreat, and the German High Command decided to relieve him. A telegram was sent to General Paul von Hindenburg, a sixty-seven-year-old soldier then in retirement, asking him if he would take over Prittwitz's army.

"I am ready," Hindenburg replied, and he went to the eastern front accompanied by Erich Ludendorff, the hero of Liège. Thus was formed the

Charles Fouqueray painted this vivid scene of men of the B.E.F. charging into battle oblivious of their wounds or their fallen comrades—oblivious too, it seems, of their heavy packs and lack of helmets. One British officer wrote with some surprise: "Real bullets were flying about, real shells . . . fired. Somebody was aiming at us."

BALTIC
SEA

KURLAND

Riga

LITHUANIA

Dvinsk

N

Königsberg

Kovno

Vilna

FIRST

EAST
PRUSSIA

Danzig

GERMANY

Masurian
Lakes

Grodno

Minsk

RUSSIA

Ger.
EIGHTH

Tannenberg

Mlawa

Narew R.

Toruń

SECOND

POLAND

Bug R.

Niemen R.

Brest Litovsk

PRIPET
MARSHES

Posen

Oder R.

Warsaw

Vistula

Lodz

Breslau

Ivangorod

Lublin

Kholm

FOURTH

FIFTH

THIRD

SILESIA

Aus.
FIRST

Tarnów

San R.

Rava
Russkaya

Kiev

BOHEMIA

Kraków

GALICIA

Jaroslaw

Lemberg

EIGHTH

UKRAINE

Aus.
FOURTH

Gorlice

Przemyśl

Dniester R.

Sept. 26

DUKLA
PASS

Aus.
THIRD

CARPATHIAN
MTS.

LUPKOW PASS
UZHOK PASS

Aus.
SECOND

Vienna

Czernowitz

Budapest

BUCOVINA

Dniester R.

AUSTRIA-HUNGARY

TRANSYLVANIA

Odessa

Sava R.

Danube R.

AUSTRIAN

Belgrade

BLACK
SEA

BOSNIA

Šabac

SERBIAN

Bucharest

RUMANIA

Sarajevo

Jadar R.

Drina R.

SERBIA

BULGARIA

Constanta

MONTENEGRO

Sofia

BALKAN MTS.

Varna

ADRIATIC
SEA

Scale

0   30   60   90 Miles

famous Hindenburg-Ludendorff team. Stolid and imposing like Joffre, but so dull-witted that he could boast of never having read a book since he left school, Hindenburg would rely more and more upon his brilliant deputy. Ludendorff, eighteen years younger than his chief, would seize more and more power until this monstrously ambitious man would become the virtual dictator of Germany.

On the Russian front that summer, Hindenburg and Ludendorff took things in hand and prepared a great victory. Although they were outnumbered, by more than 2 to 1, they knew that the Russian Army was poorly led and was in the habit of outrunning its supply columns. After they saw that the Russian First Army in the north was moving slowly, they decided to turn on the Second Army in the south under General Alexander Samsonov.

While one German force held Samsonov's center in place, two others began biting at his flanks. Left and right, the Germans drove the Russians back. Now the Russian center was exposed on either side. The Germans closed around it. They surrounded Samsonov's center. The maneuver called double envelopment, made famous by Hannibal's great victory over the Romans at Cannae, had been brilliantly executed by Hindenburg and Ludendorff, and on August 31 Hindenburg, in a triumphant mood, cabled the Kaiser:

"I beg most humbly to report to Your Majesty that the ring round the larger part of the Russian Army was closed yesterday. The 13th, and 15th and [23rd] Army Corps have been destroyed. We have already taken more than sixty thousand prisoners, among them the Corps Commanders of the 13th and 15th Corps. The guns are still in the forest and are now being brought in. The booty is immense though it cannot yet be assessed in detail. The Corps outside our ring, the 1st and 6th, have also suffered severely and are now retreating in hot haste through Mlawa and Myszaniec."

Russia had been struck a stunning blow. Gen-

SÜDDEUTSCHER VERLAG, MUNICH

Hindenburg watches the Battle of Tannenberg through a field periscope as Ludendorff (third from left) stands by.

eral Samsonov vanished into the forests, where, it is believed, he killed himself. And Hindenburg called his victory the Battle of Tannenberg, to efface the shame of another Tannenberg, at which the Poles and the Lithuanians had defeated the Teutonic Knights in 1410.

Although Tannenberg was not a decisive loss for the Russians, it would have changed the entire war completely if the Germans had lost it. Moreover, it was to have a profound influence on the battle then raging in the West.

On August 25, the very day on which General Joffre realized that the main German offensive was already pouring south from Belgium, an aide of General Moltke's decided that the victory was already won. As a result, he proposed to withdraw six corps from the western front and send them to East Prussia. At that time, the Germans facing Russia appeared to be losing. Eventually, only two corps were ordered east. But they were taken from the vital German right wing, which had already been weakened because it had had to post guards in the conquered cities left behind. In all, the right wing was down from thirty-four to twenty-five divisions. Nevertheless, the French were not aware of this.

The map at left traces three early engagements on the eastern front: the Russian defeat at Tannenberg, to the north; the German advance and retreat in Galicia, at center; and the Austrian bridgehead in Serbia, to the south.

25

L'ILLUSTRATION

MUSEE DE LA GUERRE, PARIS

DEPT. OF THE ARMY

In the early months of the war, each day brought thousands of new casualties. Above, wounded British marines leave Antwerp in October, 1914. Among all survivors was a deep sense of loneliness, as reflected in the painting at right, above, of German prisoners of war. The sketch at right shows a lone German dragging a comrade to safety.

Russian soldiers surrender at Tannenberg (above).
Below, Russian prisoners rest in a Galician field.

They knew only that Paris and all of France were in peril. Kluck and Bülow were driving remorselessly down toward the capital. Kluck, commanding the German's westmost prong, was to swing around the city; Bülow, just inside of him to the east, would march against it.

In front of Kluck the B.E.F. was in full retreat; in front of Bülow the French Fifth Army was closer to a rout.

On August 25, to help defend the city, the French formed the Sixth Army under General Michel Joseph Maunoury.

But on the same day, Sir John French notified Lord Kitchener in London that he intended to withdraw to the southwest. In effect, he was pulling out of the war.

Even so, almost at the same time, the German commanders began to make blunders of their own. On August 25, Kluck decided he would wheel inward, coming even closer to Bülow. This meant that instead of going west around Paris and then wheeling east *below* it to scoop the city into the German net, he was turning east *above* it. He was going to slide by.

27

He made his fatal turn on August 31. A British aviator observed it and reported it, but as yet the French did not react.

Defeat and retreat were the order of the day. On September 2, Joffre advised the Ministry of War: "All our hopes are defeated. We are in full retreat all along the line. Maunoury's army is falling back on Paris." The Government fled. General Joseph Simon Gallieni, Commander of Paris, prepared to fight. He was willing to reduce beautiful Paris to rubble rather than surrender it to the Germans.

Lord Kitchener had already rushed over from London to confront Sir John French in a painful scene and order him to keep the B.E.F. in action. Sir John obeyed, although he continued his backward movement. It was a black night for France; and then, in General Gallieni's staff room, additional reports of Kluck's eastward turn were received and pinned up on a map. Two French colonels ob-

L'ILLUSTRATION

Sir John French (center) described as "amiable enough, though petulant when thwarted" seems about to stamp his foot in impatience as he listens to a lecture delivered by Joffre. Apparently amused, Sir Douglas Haig observes at right.

served it, and with one voice they cried out joyously:

"They offer us their flank! They offer us their flank!"

It was true. By turning to his left, Kluck had exposed his right wing. General Gallieni saw it at once. He rushed to Joffre and pointed out the golden opportunity. If he held all the way along the line he could swing his left against the Germans and get around them. All would depend on the French Sixth Army on the far left and its nearest right-hand neighbor: Sir John French and his B.E.F.

Joffre got his Sixth Army moving. He went to see Sir John, of whose intentions he was still not sure. He begged him to co-operate.

"Monsieur le Maréchal," he said, "it is France who beseeches you."

Sir John tried to stammer his reply in French. Failing to make himself understood, he turned to an officer and exclaimed:

"Dammit, I can't explain! Tell him that all that men can do our fellows will do."

Joffre returned to his headquarters relieved, and thus was begun the famous Battle of the Marne. It raged for seven days on a broad front from Verdun to Meaux. It was a compound of large clashes and small skirmishes, of heroism and stupidity, of lightning rallies and lost opportunities. At one point, Maunoury's Sixth Army on the left was in danger of being overwhelmed in its lunge to get around Kluck. In Paris, Gallieni rounded up reinforcements, loaded them into twelve hundred taxicabs and sent his famous "Taxicab Army" rattling to the rescue.

In the center, the *poilus*—"hairy ones"—of the French Fifth Army fought like lions, now that they had a new commander. General Louis Franchet d'Esperey was one of the greatest French leaders of the war, and he inspired his men to halt the Germans of Bülow's army and send them reeling back.

And on Franchet d'Esperey's own right an even more brilliant French commander entered history. General Ferdinand Foch led the new Ninth Army, which Joffre had formed. Counterattacking steadily, Foch's men exhausted the German Third Army opposing them. It is then that this little, bandy-legged leader is supposed to have signaled Joffre: "My right gives. My center yields. Situation excellent. I attack!" What is true is even more impressive. Foch

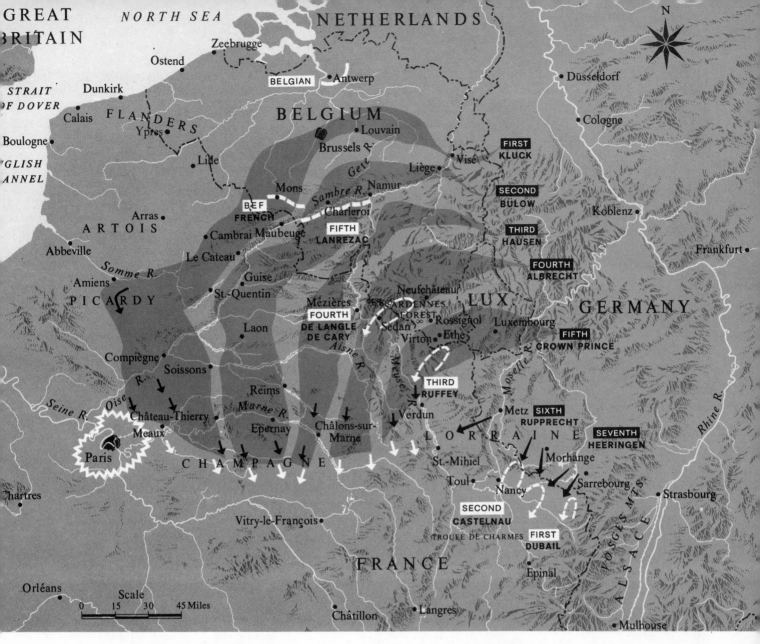

German armies cut a wide swath (gray area) through France to the Marne in August, 1914. There the British and French troops held and later rallied to push the Germans back.

had judged that in attacking the French flanks the German commander had stripped his center. So the French plunged straight ahead and cracked the German middle.

Now it was Sir John French's chance. A gap had opened and then widened between Kluck and Bülow. Sir John's forces were directly opposite it. If he plunged in, he could split the enemy in two. But Sir John French dawdled, and by the time Joffre could get him to move, it was too late.

Far away in Luxembourg, General Moltke was in a state of near collapse. His shining dream, his great victory, was vanishing with the defeat of his armies. Paris was not going to be netted, nor was France going to fall that summer. Instead, the Kaiser's finest were in danger of defeat. General Moltke granted a colonel the power to do what he dared not: to sound a full retreat.

Back to the Aisne River went the stunned Germans. There they turned again and dug in. The Battle of the Marne—what the French call "the Miracle of the Marne"—had stemmed the field-gray tide.

Relieved, though far from jubilant, the French Government came back to Paris.

THE WORLD AT WAR

The defeat at the Marne ended the career of Helmuth von Moltke. It sank him so deep into a sickly gloom that he had to be relieved by General Erich von Falkenhayn, an energetic and ruthless soldier who immediately attempted to get around, or "turn," the French seaward flank.

But General Joseph Joffre was also trying to turn the Germans on their seaward side. Both generals were attempting one of the basic maneuvers of warfare, that is, the flanking, or turning, movement. Much like an end run in football, a flanking movement aims at getting around the enemy's end, or flank, so as to strike him in the rear and chop his forces into pieces (see map on page 32).

Thus, when the hostile armies attempted this, they both began lunging toward the coast. This part of the war was known as the Race to the Sea. As it was going on, the Germans were also driving King Albert of Belgium out of his stronghold in Antwerp. Albert retreated to the little town of Nieuport on the North Sea. When he did, he linked up with the Anglo-French forces on his right. Soon after, the pursuing Germans came to a halt opposite him. Thus, the Race to the Sea had ended in a tie. The German right was firmly anchored at the water's edge, and so was the Allied left; and the same situation existed at the other end of the western front, where the opposing flanks rested on the mountains of neutral Switzerland.

The battle line had now been drawn. It ran for four hundred miles, from the North Sea down through a corner of Belgium and across France to Switzerland. It was now not possible to turn the enemy's flank. The "end run" was out, and the only maneuver possible—or so the generals thought—was the "penetration," or straight-ahead line plunge.

The Germans tried it first and the place they chose was Ypres.

The British were holding this ancient little Belgian town with the difficult name. "Wipers," the Tommies called it, and one day the Yanks would call it "Yeeps." The Germans wanted it because it was a communications hub. Their roads ran into it, and out of it ran roads to valuable ports. Ypres was also an Allied salient, that is, a bulge inside the German line. This was another reason for wanting to take it.

For four years millions of men would struggle for this little city surrounded by tiny villages with heavy Flemish names. In all, a million men were to suffer death or wounds at Ypres, until the city would be known as Ypres, la Morte: the City of the Dead.

On October 20, the First Battle of Ypres began. The gray German lines rushed forward. For ten days they battered at the British, and then, just as the British line was breaking, they withdrew. They came again in November, until at last the violence of their onslaught expired amid howling blizzards.

The Allies also tried attacking. Field Marshal Sir John French, assisted by two French divisions, tried to gain a foothold north of the Germans. But he was stopped by a counterattack.

First Ypres became distinguished by much blood and agony and much bombast. The Kaiser himself came forward to cheer his men on, and Sir John French is supposed to have told General Ferdinand Foch, "All that remains for me to do is to get

The Dutch artist Louis Raemaekers portrayed Kaiser Wilhelm gripped by the skeletons of War and Hunger. His cartoons helped to rouse the world against German brutality.

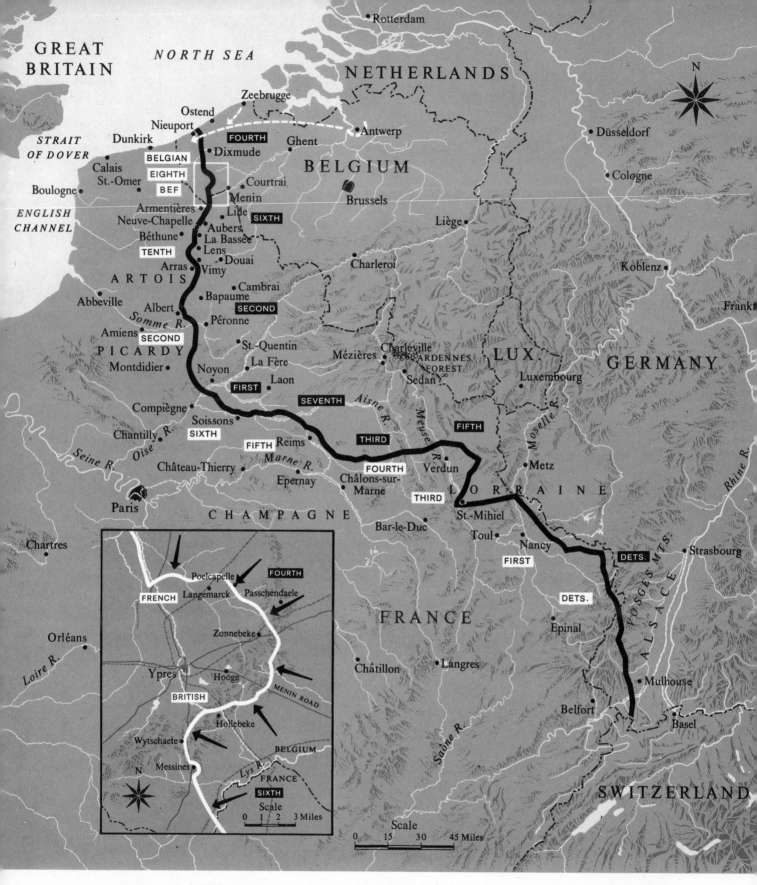

GREAT
BRITAIN

NORTH SEA

NETHERLANDS

• Rotterdam

• Zeebrugge

Ostend •

Nieuport •

*STRAIT
OF DOVER*

Dunkirk •

Dixmude •

FOURTH

Ghent •

• Antwerp

BELGIUM

• Düsseldorf

• Cologne

Calais •

St.-Omer •

BELGIAN

EIGHTH

BEF

• Courtrai

Menin •

Brussels •

Liège •

• Koblenz

Boulogne •

*ENGLISH
CHANNEL*

Armentières •

Lille •

Neuve-Chapelle •

Aubers •

SIXTH

• Frank

Béthune •

La Bassée •

Lens •

TENTH

Arras •

Vimy •

• Douai

ARTOIS

• Charleroi

Abbeville •

Albert •

Cambrai •

Bapaume •

SECOND

• Péronne

LUX.

GERMANY

Somme R.

Amiens •

SECOND

PICARDY

• St.-Quentin

Montdidier •

Noyon •

La Fère •

Mézières •

ARDENNES
FOREST

Charleville

Sedan •

Luxembourg •

FIRST

Laon •

Aisne R.

Meuse R.

Compiègne •

SEVENTH

FIFTH

Moselle R.

Soissons •

THIRD

Chantilly •

Oise R.

SIXTH

Reims •

Marne R.

FIFTH

Verdun •

• Metz

Rhine R.

Seine R.

Château-Thierry •

FOURTH

Epernay •

Châlons-sur-
Marne

LORRAINE

THIRD

St.-Mihiel •

Paris •

CHAMPAGNE

Bar-le-Duc •

Toul •

• Strasbourg

Chartres •

FRANCE

Nancy •

DETS.

FIRST

VOSGES MTS.

DETS.

Châtillon •

Langres •

Epinal •

ALSACE

Loire R.

Orléans •

• Mulhouse

Saône R.

Belfort •

Basel •

SWITZERLAND

Inset map:

FRENCH

Poelcapelle •

FOURTH

Langemarck •

Passchendaele •

Zonnebeke •

Ypres •

Hooge •

BRITISH

MENIN ROAD

Hollebeke •

Wytschaete •

BELGIUM

Messines •

Lys R.

FRANCE

SIXTH

N

Scale
0   1   2   3 Miles

Scale
0   15   30   45 Miles

*By December, 1914, the opposing armies on the western front had dug in along a 400-mile line from the
North Sea to the Swiss border. The series of maneuvers that established the line in Belgium was called the
Race to the Sea. A major battle in the German attempt to break through the line was at Ypres (inset).*

killed," and to have been told in reply: "You must not talk of dying but of winning." But the men in the mud were dying, and no one was winning. "The breakthrough will be decisive," a German general told his divisions, but there was no breakthrough.

There was only an exodus and a ruin. German artillery took little Ypres apart, church by shop, mansion by wretched hovel, hospital by schoolhouse. Gothic towers came crashing down, and medieval masterpieces were shattered into shards. The townspeople fled, and the town became a warren of rubble inhabited by those poor rabbity orphans or demented widows who could not flee. Ypres had been the first city to feel the rumbling wrath of this horrible new warfare, foreshadowing the doom of other places that were luckless enough to be militarily desirable.

Also foreshadowed was the dreadful loss of human life that was to be characteristic of World War I. The gray German tides flowed into the merciless rifle fire of the British and were cut to pieces, while the Tommies, lying in poorly protected positions, were shredded by German artillery. First Ypres cost the Germans 130,000 soldiers; the British lost about 60,000, and the French about the same. In all, there had been a quarter of a million casualties, and from this the generals, seeing only that the battle lines had not been altered, came to the conclusion that they needed more munitions.

At that time, England was only making 30,000 artillery shells a month. Within less than a year she would be manufacturing 1,200,000 shells monthly. France's output would also skyrocket, as would that of Germany.

And all these munitions would be used to kill and maim millions of men and wreck the countryside in a war that the generals would never understand. They were too far back, in comfortable châteaux or safe cities, to know what was happening.

Both sides, fearing enemy shellfire, were digging deeper and deeper. As they did, more and more artillery was emplaced by either side. They either battered the enemy's trenchworks—usually doing no more than forcing him to dig deeper—or they laid down barrages to precede infantry attacks. These bombardments chewed up the middle ground between opposing armies, making that famous no man's land of shell-pocked mud. Troops moving to the attack had rough going through no man's land. After their own artillery barrage lifted, they were exposed to the enemy's artillery. If they got through, they had only reached the enemy's barbed wire—and here they were usually cut to pieces by interlocking machine gun fire.

Thus, infantry could never close with infantry, and there could be no decisive result. There was only deadlock, a bloody red agonizing stalemate. Hearing of the carnage at Ypres, Lord Kitchener cried: "This isn't war!"

It may not have been, by his lordship's nineteenth-century standards, but the mud-streaked, lice-ridden, miserable moles of both sides knew it as war—the most futile and frustrating ever fought. Worse, it was now engulfing the entire globe.

A country's geography often shapes her history. Switzerland has been able to remain neutral

RAEMAEKERS, *The Great War,* 1916

Raemaekers' The Very Stones Cry Out *denounces the shelling of Reims Cathedral (background). Two church statues point accusingly at a German soldier.*

Across the shell-pocked battlefield move stretcher bearers carrying a wounded comrade. This sketch of the area between trenches was made by Georges Victor-Hugo, grandson of the novelist.

because passage across her rugged mountains is much more difficult than, say, traversing the level Belgian plain. Turkey, on the other hand, is one of the world's oldest battlegrounds.

Turkey controls the Dardanelles, the vital straits linking the Black Sea with the Mediterranean. Russia has always coveted the Dardanelles. They would give her an exit into warm waters. Down the Straits would go Russia's exports of grain and up them would come imports of industrial goods. This would be especially true in war, and that was why it was to the interest of the Allies to keep the Dardanelles open and why it was the concern of the Central Powers to block them (see inset map on page 47).

Germany, alert to the importance of the Straits, had been courting Turkey for years. German generals were placed in command of the Turkish Army, Turks in field gray and *Pickelhauben* (spiked helmets) learned the Prussian goose step, and German engineers helped fortify the Straits. Moreover, the Germans had the ear of the corrupt men who ruled the Turkish people.

Chief of these was a former mailman and telegrapher with the build of a heavyweight wrestler. His name was Talaat Pasha. His second in command was a foppish young man named Enver Pasha. These were the men who tortured and robbed and carried out wholesale massacres of Armenians and other minority groups while flirting dangerously with the Germans.

While German influence in Turkey increased, England, the great seafaring power that had always understood the importance of the Dardanelles, made no attempt to interfere. For decades England had been the self-appointed "guardian" of that floundering Turkish Empire that was known as the Sick Man of Europe. England, however, had grown too confident of her ability to control the Turks. Then, as war neared, England made a most unwise —and unjust—move.

Winston Churchill, then First Lord of the Admiralty, requisitioned two big battleships being built for Turkey in English shipyards. The Turks were enraged. Money to buy these ships had been raised

34

By March, 1915, networks of trenches like the one in the oil painting above had become homes as well as fortresses for the front line troops. Passages were narrow, but taller than the men who moved through them. Huts were carved out of dirt walls, and planks extended across the trenches to provide roofs.

by the people. Talaat and Enver fanned the flames of hatred against England, and then they proposed a secret treaty with Germany and began mobilizing.

England, unaware of the secret pact, offered Turkey a promise that none of the Allies, including Russia, would molest her if she would stay neutral. Turkey refused. The German ambassador was already telling the Turks what a traitor England had been and what a friend Germany would be. As proof, Germany ordered two cruisers in the Mediterranean to Constantinople. The *Goeben* and *Bres-*

lau would compensate for the battleships that the British had taken.

The British fleet attempted to intercept the cruisers. A thrilling chase began in the Mediterranean. The accounts of the pursuit make fascinating reading. The *Goeben* sighted! The *Goeben* pursued! The *Goeben* slipping away . . .

Both the *Goeben* and the *Breslau* got clean away. They sailed up the Straits past the silent guns of the Turkish forts. Now the Germans pressed Enver Pasha: "If the English ships follow, shall the forts fire on them?" Enver Pasha thought a moment, and replied: "Yes."

A farce was begun, to maintain the appearance of a "neutral" Turkey. It was pretended that Turkey had bought the ships from Germany. German sailors took off their flat tops and put on Turkish fezzes. Talaat and Enver were still cautious about offending the Allies. They wanted to see how the war went before they made their move. At first it seemed to be going well for the Germans. Russia had been beaten at Tannenberg, and the Germans were sweeping through Belgium into France.

One day a Turkish diplomat stopped a visiting Belgian on a street in Constantinople and said: "I have terrible news for you. The Germans have captured Brussels."

"I have more terrible news for you," the Belgian replied. "The Germans have captured Turkey."

It was true. For all intents and purposes, the Germans were running things. Then, as the Turks seemed to waver after the defeat of the Germans at the Marne, the German Navy put an end to the masquerade. On October 29, the *Goeben* and *Breslau* sailed up the Straits into the Black Sea. They entered the Russian port of Odessa where they sank a Russian gunboat, shelled a French freighter, and subjected a sugar factory to bombardment, wrecking it and killing many Russian workers.

Talaat and Enver dropped the mask. They came out openly for Germany and closed the Dardanelles to Russia. They exchanged declarations of war with the Allies, and eventually another half of the world would be drawn into the war. Turkey's neighbors—Bulgaria, Rumania, Italy, and Greece—would come in. Allied strength would be drawn off into campaigns of the Dardanelles, Suez, Mesopotamia, and Palestine. Turkey herself would suffer cruelly for the gamble taken by her racketeering rulers. The ancient Ottoman Empire would break up, and Turkey would lose nearly a quarter of her population. Starvation and disease would rack the home front, while Allied arms would scourge the armies raised by Talaat and Enver.

All this would proceed from the voyage of the German cruisers. Worst of all for the Allies—and the world—Russia would be paralyzed. With the Straits closed to her, Russia's exports dropped by 98 per cent and her imports by 95 per cent. She had neither the goods of war nor the money to pay for them. Within a year, Russian soldiers would march off to war without cartridges. Two more years, and Czarist power would totally collapse—and the red rage of Communism would enter history.

Meanwhile, the empire that had started the war that wrecked empires was itself tottering.

Eight nations, seventeen countries, twenty parliamentary groups, twenty-seven political parties, and languages and dialects by the dozen—that was the Austrian Empire, or Austria-Hungary, as it

General Franz Conrad von Hötzendorf, Commander in Chief of the Austrian Army, inspects his troops in Galicia.

WELTKRIEGSBÜCHEREI, STUTTGART

36

King Peter of Serbia (seated) watches his little army drive the Austrians from Serbian soil.

was also called. It was "a melting pot on a cold fire." Three quarters of the officers in the Austrian Army were of German stock, but only one soldier in four spoke German. Often a platoon leader could not make himself understood by his men. Moreover, many of the men would have no wish to obey the orders of an empire that they hated, given in the language they detested.

Without a unified army, Austria-Hungary had no hope of winning even the "bright, brisk little war" that had been so optimistically envisioned by General Franz Conrad von Hötzendorf.

Conrad, a reckless plunger, went charging north to get at the Russians. But the southern group of Russian armies had better leaders than the northern group, which had been beaten at Tannenberg. Conrad's forces were lured deep into Poland, and then the Russians began swinging at his flanks. The right wing was sent backpedaling toward Austria, and Conrad's forces were driven backward in humiliating retreat.

In the south, another Austrian army was humbled by little Serbia. Two months later General Conrad tried to efface the shame of that defeat, but received the same treatment himself. Serbia, for the sake of whose land Austria-Hungary had plunged the world into untold devastation, had successfully defied her bullying neighbor.

Moreover, Austria-Hungary's military weakness had been made plain to the world. She might have served her German ally better if she had remained on guard within her natural defenses. Kaiser Wilhelm was faced with the choice of propping up his sick partner or letting him fall. He chose the first alternative, of course, but that gave rise to its own problems. As German officers were to say: "We are fettered to a corpse."

So ended the first year of the Great War. The leaves of autumn had fallen, but the Kaiser's troops were still not home. The snows of winter were falling now, and they made mounds of the corpses of soldiers sprawled across the face of Europe.

The sketch above by Herbert Hillier shows salvos from a British ship pounding the Turkish positions at Gallipoli. At the far right is the entrance to the Dardanelles.

THE DARDANELLES 4

Winston Churchill has usually been credited with having conceived the idea of forcing the Turkish Straits. But the proposal first came from Churchill's fierce old First Sea Lord, Admiral Sir John Fisher.

Fisher thought British battleships could force the Straits and so clear the path to Constantinople and Russia beyond. But then he began to cool on his plan, and as fast as he did, Churchill began to warm to it. Eventually, the persuasive Churchill convinced Britain's leaders to adopt what was to be a combined land-sea assault.

This narrow, strategically vital watery passage was once called the Hellespont. It was renamed the Dardanelles. Entering it, on the right hand lies Asiatic Turkey, the land mass also known in history as Asia Minor. On the left is European Turkey and the long strip of land called the Gallipoli Peninsula (see pages 46–47). On Gallipoli had been built the forts mounting the guns that commanded the Straits. Churchill's plan called for Allied warships to batter these and force their way up to Constantinople.

On February 19, 1915, Admiral Sir Sackville Carden's fleet began blasting away at the forts from long range. They were so successful that shore parties of marines and sailors were able to land on Gallipoli and blow the guns on the heights at the entrance. The Straits were heavily mined, however. Civilian crews manning the mine sweepers refused to brave the dangers of sweeping for mines close to shore. Inexperienced sailors were drafted for the mission, which they handled poorly and which wasted time.

It was now March 15, and Britain had decided to storm Gallipoli as well as to force the Dardanelles. Lord Kitchener called in General Sir Ian Hamilton and said: "We are sending a military force to support the fleet now at the Dardanelles, and you are to have command." With no plan and no balanced staff to make one, Sir Ian rushed off to the scene.

In the meantime, Admiral Carden had become ill, and command of the fleet fell to Vice-Admiral Sir John Michael de Robeck. On March 18, de Robeck's ships stood off the entrance and began bombarding Fort Chanak guarding the Narrows. A French squadron—the *Bouvet, Charlemagne, Gaulois,* and *Suffren*—joined the cannonading, Fort Chanak fell silent, and de Robeck sent six battleships steaming into the Straits. On they came—the *Majestic, Albion, Irresistible, Ocean, Swiftsure,* and *Vengeance*—the Dreadnoughts of the line. But the guns of the Turkish fort had not been put out of commission. Now, with the narrow channel crowded with big ships, they began to thunder.

The *Bouvet* was hit and sank quickly with most of her crew. The *Irresistible* hit a mine and lasted for slightly more than an hour. The *Ocean* blundered into another mine and went under with a roar and a hiss, and the *Gaulois* and *Inflexible* were badly battered. Still, the Anglo-French heavies slugged on. Only with dark did they withdraw.

Admiral de Robeck expected to return to the assault. But in the meantime, Sir Ian Hamilton had wired Lord Kitchener that he believed the Straits could not be forced by battleships alone. It was, in fact, none of General Hamilton's business. It was a matter for the admirals to decide. But his report had done its mischief. Admiral de Robeck was forced to agree with General Hamilton, the fleet withdrew, and Britain prepared to take the Gallipoli Peninsula by storm.

All of the high commanders on the western front were opposed to the venture at Gallipoli. They thought it drew strength away from the West, where, they argued, the victory must be won. To prove that point Field Marshal Sir John French staged an attack at Neuve-Chapelle, just below Ypres. Sir John wanted a penetration, and Neuve-Chapelle would be the first of the line-plunges seeking it.

On March 10, the British under Sir Douglas Haig attacked on a short two-mile front. Three days later it was over, and it had failed. Penetration had been achieved—one of the three times it was done in the West—but it could not be exploited. Troops who did get to the German rear were unable to notify their commanders that they were there. After the Germans began hammering the Allied flanks, it was impossible to rush support into the bulge. So the attack failed, and its chief result was to make the Gallipoli campaign seem even more desirable.

On the eastern front the Germans were having difficulties of their own: a family squabble. Hindenburg and Ludendorff had made no bones of their contempt for the new Chief of Staff, General Falkenhayn. They wanted his job. Throughout the winter of 1914–15, the Kaiser himself had had to act as the referee in the dispute. Then, in February, 1915, Hindenburg and Ludendorff attempted to execute a double-pronged offensive against the Russians. If they brought it off, their prestige would soar. The idea was for General Conrad to strike out from Galicia in the south with his Austrians, and for Hindenburg and Ludendorff to attack from the north in Prussia. "Our thrusting wings were to surround the enemy," wrote Ludendorff, "and the sooner the better."

But there were too many Russians and too much snow. The Austrians in the south got nowhere, and although the Germans in the north did succeed in destroying the Russian Tenth Army—capturing 110,000 soldiers and hundreds of guns—they were unable to knock Russia out of the war.

April 22, 1915, was a lovely day at Ypres. Allied soldiers basked in a mild spring sun. A gentle breeze blowing from the German trenches caressed their faces. They forgot the horror of the preceding forty-eight hours, when the Germans had battered Ypres with the Big Berthas that had crushed Liège.

But, then, at five o'clock sharp, the mortars rumbled again. A hissing sound issued from the German lines. Suddenly, opposite the village of Langemarck, held by French Colonials, two greenish-yellow clouds appeared. They merged and began rolling

forward over five miles of front. Some soldiers were enchanted by the unearthly beauty of the clouds rolling low like a glistening fog over the wastes of no man's land. Others were afraid.

Then the mists swept over them, choking them, inflicting upon them slow death or disability—shattering their wills and forcing them to panic.

The Germans had introduced poison gas into the arsenal of war. They had chosen to loose their deadly chlorine cloud on African troops, who fled its choking coils in dread, leaving a gap of four and a half miles in the Ypres front. Battalions of Canadians fought bravely to plug the gap. Behind them, there was panic in Ypres.

"Children wailed, and men's voices cursed and growled in uncouth *Flamand* accents," an eyewitness wrote. "The sky seemed a vault of flame, and the tall budding poplar trees . . . rustled and whistled eerily in the wind."

Ghastly and diabolical as the attack had been, the Germans were not able to exploit their advantage. Some commanders distrusted the new weapon, and most of the advance troops feared to get too close to it. And the deathless courage of the Canadian division and of two British battalions that were rushed to the front eventually closed the gap.

Nevertheless, the horrible genie was out of the bottle. In self-defense, the Allies would also resort to gas warfare. More and more deadly mixtures would be developed. Troops of both sides would be issued gas masks. Ugly and stifling contraptions that they were, men who wanted to live had to put them on when they heard that chilling cry: "Gas!"

If I should die, think only this of me:
That there's some corner of a foreign field
That is for ever England.

Thus wrote Rupert Brooke, the brave and handsome young poet who has been called "the symbolic figure in the Gallipoli campaign." Rupert Brooke did die, of blood poisoning just before the battle; and he was buried on a foreign field—the island of Skyros—as thousands of English, French, Australians, and New Zealanders were to die and be buried on the cheerless soil of Gallipoli.

CONTINUED ON PAGE 45

In 1915, a horrible new dimension was added to warfare when the Germans introduced the use of gas. Exploded by firing cylinders, chlorine gas floated over the trenches, filling the lungs of its victims and causing suffocation. To protect the soldiers, a variety of masks were developed, such as the snout-faced respirators in the painting at right. As the war progressed, both sides developed new gases. The most terrifying was mustard gas, introduced by the Germans in 1917. It caused severe burning of the skin and was particularly dangerous to the eyes. In the photograph at left, soldiers blinded by gas shuffle into an advanced dressing station near Béthune in April, 1918.

MUSEE DE LA GUERRE, PARIS

Several months of indecisive battles led to a stalemate on the western front at the end of 1914.

War left its mark on every battlefield in Europe. Above are German casualties in France.

Winston Churchill and Admiral Jack Fisher (above) leave a meeting of the Committee of Imperial Defence. Together they planned a naval attack on the Dardanelles. When this failed, troops were sent to attempt a landing. At left, Anzacs line the decks of a ship steaming toward the Gallipoli shore.

General Hamilton led seventy thousand men against eighty-four thousand Turks under the German General Otto Liman von Sanders. The main Allied force was divided into two groups. One, under Major General Sir Aylmer G. Hunter-Weston was to seize the tip of the peninsula at the entrance to the Straits. This right-hand group was made up of English and French. On the left, the Australian–New Zealand Army Corps (Anzacs) under General Sir William Birdwood would land at a place later to be known as Anzac Cove. Both forces were to march inland to the high ground.

The Anzacs were to land first in the early-morning darkness of April 25. They arrived in battleships and destroyers and got into small boats for the land-ing. In the dark their order was scrambled, and they landed about a mile to the left of their objective.

Still, there were only two Turkish rifle companies to oppose the eight thousand Anzacs safely ashore. However, messengers had already gone panting away in search of a colonel named Mustafa Kemal. One day he would go into history as Atatürk, "Chief Turk," the founder of modern Turkey. On this day he heard the news of the landing, and snapped to his soldiers: "Have we got ball cartridges? All right, follow me." Off they went—five hundred of them—to seize the heights of Chunuk Bair just as a few Australians were climbing it. Kemal's men beat them back. More Anzacs came charging into the battle with that high-hearted swaggering zest that is theirs alone. But the Turks were building up forces too. On and on the critical fight raged, but by night-fall Kemal and his men still held Chunuk Bair.

The decisive battle of the campaign had been fought. Even though sixteen thousand Anzacs were to come ashore at Anzac Cove, they were crowded into a tight little crescent and raked by artillery fire plunging down from Chunuk. And on the right at the beachhead called Cape Helles, the Allied cause was also floundering.

Here General Hunter-Weston began five land-ings. From left to right they were on beaches called Y, X, W, V, and S. The main stroke was aimed at beaches W and V. At V-Beach a troop-loaded col-lier, the *River Clyde*, was deliberately beached. Bunched masses of Tommies came boiling out of the broached vessel—straight into the stuttering guns of the Turks. It was a slaughter.

At W-Beach, the spearheads came ashore in small boats. The Turks held their fire until the boats were close. Then they opened up with a roar and there was a bloody duplication of V-Beach.

There was no guard at X-Beach, and those troops quickly dug in. They were to be the reserve.

Only a few Turks held S-Beach and they fled be-fore the Allied onslaught. But the Allied soldiers merely stayed put. They could have marched around to the Turkish rear and struck at the troops firing on the *River Clyde*. But they did not.

The troops who landed at Y-Beach on the extreme left could have done the same. But they also daw-dled. Thus, the golden chance was allowed to slip

45

GALLIPOLI CAMPAIGN

March 1915 — January 1916

TURKEY

SAROS GULF ②

Bula

GALLIPOLI

Aug. 7-8

Aug. 7

LIMAN VON SANDERS

Anafarta Sagir

SCIMITAR HILL

HILL 971

CHUNUK BAIR ⑦

Final Line

LONE PINE

AZMAK DERE

Aug. 8

Salt Lake

CHOCOLATE HILL

ARI BURNU

ANZAC ⑤ *Anzac Cove*

IX ⑧

SUVLA BAY

BIRDWOOD

GABA TEPE

STOPFORD

AEGEAN SEA

HAMILTON

KRITHIA TO BULAIR, 39 MILES

David Greenspan

An Allied fleet attack in March, 1915, failed to force the Dardanelles (1). On April 25, diversionary thrusts at the Gulf of Saros (2) and Kum Kale (3) protected troop landings at Cape Helles (4) and Ari Burnu (5). First-day toe holds (white dots) on X-, W-, V-, and S-beaches were enlarged to a unified beachhead by early May. On August 6, the Turks withstood an Allied attack at Helles (6) and rushed troops (broken black arrows) to repel an Anzac lunge (7, white arrows) at Chunuk Bair. Turks also met the August 7 British landing at Suvla Bay (8). Heavily loaded lifeboats carrying the British soldiers from their transports to Suvla Bay are shown in the painting at right.

away. With their center pinned down, the Allies might have tried to swing both or either one of their wings around the Turks. But they did not.

A few days later General Hunter-Weston attempted to break out of his beachhead on the right at Cape Helles. But by then General Liman von Sanders had brought up his reserves and halted the assault. Next, Liman ordered his men to "drive the invaders into the sea" at bayonet point. But the Turkish drive was also hurled back. Another Allied attempt failed, and then began a terrible period of wasting attacks on both sides while the entrenched

forces dug in deeper. The Allies could not break out of their twin slaughter pens at Anzac Cove and Cape Helles, the Turks could not break in.

General Sir Ian Hamilton cabled home for reinforcements. In the meantime, a Turkish destroyer stole down the Straits by night and fired a torpedo into the British battleship *Goliath*. The great ship, assigned to give gunfire support to Cape Helles, sank immediately with 570 persons still aboard. German submarines joined the hunt, and the battleships *Triumph* and, twelve days later, *Majestic* went to the bottom. Allied losses were atrocious, yet the

Norman Wilkinson painted Allied troops (above) advancing under heavy fire at Suvla Bay.

High Command insisted on continuing the battle.

More troops came out from England and France, and a grand attack was planned. A third beachhead was to be seized at Suvla Bay, to the left of Anzac Cove. The men at Anzac Cove, which would then become the center of the Allied line, would also attempt to break out. On the right at Cape Helles, a holding operation would be carried out.

On August 6, with twenty-five thousand green troops going ashore at Suvla Bay, this last and most desperate attempt to seize Gallipoli began.

On the left, sheer inexperience compounded by confusion brought about a fiasco at Suvla Bay. On the right, the commander tried to do more than hold, and lost half his task force of four thousand men. In the center, the attempt to break out was "launched against positions the like of which had never been attacked before under modern conditions of warfare," according to war correspondent Ellis Ashmead-Bartlett. Even great gallantry and matchless courage could not carry the day.

More than forty thousand Allied soldiers fell during the August battling at Gallipoli, and that was the last gasp.

Fighting wore on, of course. Men continued to suffer and die. Unburied bodies lay everywhere. There was never enough water to drink, and washing could only be done in the sea under the Turkish guns. Dysentery and malaria—the twin scourges of men in trenches—claimed thousands of victims. Bloated flies swarmed over half-cleaned kitchens and latrines. They fed on corpses or on the open sores of the living.

Then came the snowfalls of winter. The first blizzard to sweep Gallipoli drowned 280 men in their trenches and froze others to death where they stood. Official England was horrified. Winston Churchill had already been forced from office as the result of the debacle, and now it was at last agreed to evacuate Gallipoli. The last Allied soldier was drawn off in January, 1916.

The Turks had won. Of a half-million Allied troops sent to Gallipoli, half of them had become battle casualties. Turkey's losses were only slightly less, but she had held the vital passage to Russia and the Black Sea.

British troops (right) cling to their narrow toe hold at Cape Helles as Turkish shell fragments explode close by.

Two Austrian sentries stand guard among the snow-capped peaks of the Alps. They scan the mountaintops for signs of Italian troops posted along the common embattled border.

EASTERN DEFEAT, WESTERN DEADLOCK

5

The spring of 1915 began auspiciously for the Allies. On May 23—just as the generals of both sides were preparing to mount their spring offensives—Italy declared war on Austria.

She would pronounce against Germany a year later, but only as a formality, for Italy's true purpose in turning on her former partners was Austrian booty. Italy sought Austrian lands along the Adriatic and in the Alps. But the Italian Army was never able to burst into either area.

Four Italian offensives in 1915 washed bloodily against "a howling wilderness of stones sharp as knives." The objective was to seize a bridgehead across the Isonzo River and so pierce the famous Ljubljana Gap opening on the Balkans. But it was not to be, and that was the war for Italy. First Battle of the Isonzo, Second, Third, Fourth . . .

A quarter of a million Italians were killed or wounded in those four battles. In all, there were to be eleven battles of the Isonzo. A great army—perhaps a million men—would be thrown away in a stupid and cruel attempt to force some of the most difficult terrain in the world. Before the war ended, Italians began to surrender en masse, crying out bitterly: "*A Roma!* Let us march on Rome!" Such was the resentment created by an inept and callous government, and on this bitter soil the rank weeds of postwar Fascism would soon flourish.

All that Italy's entry into the war meant to the Allies was that a sizable Austrian army had been drawn away from the eastern front battles with Russia. Even so, Russia got more help from the continuing squabble between General Falkenhayn and Generals Hindenburg and Ludendorff.

The German Chief of Staff, with his headquarters in France, insisted that the war would be won in the West. Hindenburg and Ludendorff, headquartered in Prussia, argued that Russia was the chief foe.

Underneath all these claims was a private dispute: Hindenburg and Ludendorff wanted Falkenhayn's job, and the Chief of Staff wanted to keep it.

While the wrangle went on, the Grand Duke Nicholas, Russia's Commander in Chief, was able to avoid encirclement by two onrushing armies. He did, however, lose half a million prisoners to the Germans. On August 6, the Russians were forced to evacuate Warsaw, and by the middle of the month the Germans were overrunning Poland (map overleaf).

In September, Ludendorff tried to surround the Grand Duke's backtracking armies once more. But Nicholas again got away, and again with very heavy losses. Ludendorff considered the campaign a victory. "We had taken a great step toward Russia's

Italian soldiers are painted in action against the Austrians.

The imposing Grand Duke Nicholas led the Russians in resisting the Germans' eastward thrust.

overthrow," he wrote later. "The Grand Duke, with his strong personality, resigned and the Czar placed himself at the head of the armies."

Ludendorff had no idea what a great step had been taken. By penetrating one hundred miles into Russian territory the Germans had begun the unraveling of the rotten fabric of Czarist Russia. And by their great slaughter of the brave but often weaponless Russian soldiers they had torn a few more strands. "We have one good weapon," Russians used to say sadly, "the living breast of the soldier." It was all too true in that bloody year of 1915, and the tide of terrified refugees sent rolling back from the border towns also helped to nourish a growing discontent throughout the country.

In the Duma—a kind of parliament that was actually a powerless debating society—fiery speeches against the Government were heard for the first time in Czarist history. Alarmed, the Czar ordered the Duma dissolved. His order caused rioting in the cities, and munition plants were struck. Now thoroughly frightened, the Czar allowed the Duma to continue sitting.

In that way the crisis passed. But it was only the

forerunner of even graver ones soon to follow.

On the western front the opposing commanders had come to different conclusions about the nature of the war. General Erich von Falkenhayn had decided:

"The English troops, in spite of undeniable bravery and endurance, have proved so clumsy in action that they will accomplish nothing decisive against the German Army *in the immediate future.*"

The last four words are important. The German Chief of Staff had seen clearly that the deadlock was unbreakable for the time being. Too much artillery, too many machine guns, placed in line after line, made penetration impossible. Because of this, Falkenhayn had allowed divisions to be shifted to the eastern front, giving the English and French a 3 to 1 superiority in men. Falkenhayn knew that even with this advantage the Allies could not break through a well-constructed defense. He therefore had the Germans expand their defenses. He did not, however, tell the Kaiser that he had recognized the stalemate. To do so would have seemed defeatist and would have cost him his job.

Both General Joffre and Sir John French were optimistic, and they had no fear of losing their commands. Of the failure at Neuve-Chapelle, Sir John's headquarters said merely: "We have learnt the lessons and shall know how to avoid mistakes." Joffre, echoing this sentiment, proposed a campaign that would "finish the war in three months."

Both Joffre and French believed the answer was more artillery, more infantry, and attacks on wider fronts. In other words, more slaughter. In May, 1915, it began again in the Artois, below Ypres.

Some three hundred thousand shells, the largest bombardment of the war so far, fell on the German positions. French *poilus* with sprigs of lilac and hawthorn in their caps surged forward almost three miles into enemy country. It looked like a walkthrough, but then the Germans recovered. Their

The areas between the broken white lines and the solid white lines on the map at right chart the retreat of the Russians during two Austro-German offensives in the summer of 1915.

BALTIC
SEA

Riga

KURLAND

Sept. 30

N

Dvinsk

July 13

LITHUANIA

May 1

FIFTH

FIFTH

Königsberg

NIEMEN

Viliya R.

Kovno

Vilna

FIRST

SECOND

Danzig

EAST
PRUSSIA

TENTH

Molodechno

TENTH

Minsk

*Masurian
Lakes*

EIGHTH

Grodno

TENTH

GERMANY

Tannenberg

TWELFTH

Narew R.

Bialystok

Niemen R.

FOURTH

RUSSIA

Toruń

TWELFTH

Mlawa

BIALOWIEZA
FOREST

THIRD

Posen

Bug R.

POLAND

FIRST

Brest Litovsk

*P R I P E T
M A R S H E S*

Oder R.

Warsaw

Skierniewice

Vistula

Breslau

NINTH

Lodz

SECOND

Ivangorod

Lublin

R.

Kholm

EIGHTH

Kiev

WOYRSCH DET.

July 13

Aus.
FIRST

FOURTH

Tarnów

San R.

BUG

Rava
Russkaya

Sept. 30

ELEVENTH

SILESIA

Kraków

Aus. FOURTH

GALICIA

Jaroslaw
Lemberg

Dnieper R.

UKRAINE

BOHEMIA

ELEVENTH

Gorlice

Przemysl

THIRD

Aus.
THIRD

C A R P A T H I A N

EIGHTH

SEVENTH

Aus.
SECOND

ELEVENTH

NINTH

Vienna

SUD

M T S.

May 1

Aus.
SEVENTH

Czernowitz

Dniester R.

Budapest

BUCOVINA

Odessa

AUSTRIA-HUNGARY

TRANSYLVANIA

BLACK
SEA

Sava R.

Danube R.

Belgrade

BOSNIA

RUMANIA

Bucharest

Constanta

Drina R.

Sarajevo

SERBIA

BULGARIA

Varna

MONTENEGRO

BALKAN MTS.

Scale

DRIATIC
SEA

Sofia

0   30   60   90 Miles

Flames consume the thatch roofs of a Polish village (above) as Austrian soldiers hurry past. Laden with arms, field packs, and bulging sacks (perhaps filled with loot), the troops continue the devastating march on the northern invasion route to Russia. Photographed below is an Austrian 30.5-cm. mortar adding punch to the drive through Galicia.

counter artillery fire prevented the French reserves from entering the battle, and their own infantry was rushed up in time to close the gaps opened by the first French rush. Three days later, torrential rains fell. General Mud had intervened on the side of the Germans, and the Artois attack began to fizzle.

On the French left, the British troops commanded by Sir Douglas Haig ran into a different difficulty. The Germans had prepared their defenses in depth. The British slugged away with frightful losses. One day's fighting cost nearly twelve thousand men. A British historian wrote: "It had been a disastrous fifteen hours of squandered heroism, unredeemed by the faintest glimmer of success."

The official report of Field Marshal Sir John French sounded quite different. It said: "First Army has pierced the enemy's line on a total front of four miles. The entire first line system of trenches has been captured on a front of 3,200 yards." It sounded like a great victory, but it signified nothing. Artois was also a bloody fiasco. One result was that General Henri Philippe Pétain emerged from it as a hero. But the fight that won him fame cost France four hundred thousand soldiers. The nation was horrified at this toll. President Raymond Poincaré visited the front and heard this plea from a corps commander: "Pray do what you can to stop these local offensives. The instrument of victory is being broken in our hands." Georges Clemenceau, the Tiger of France, predicted: "If things keep going this way, there will be a revolt of the Generals against the High Command."

Things did keep going that way. "I am nibbling them," Papa Joffre blandly explained. Perhaps true, but he was also whittling away his own forces. Although he claimed that German losses equaled his own, they were only half as great.

All was not death and agony on the western front, however. Position warfare began to have a rosier side. By mutual agreement certain parts of the front became "quiet sectors." Here, whole divisions would be brought from the "noisy sectors" to rest. Beyond the sound of guns, fed on fresh cheeses, sausage, white bread, and low-priced wines, the men thought they were in paradise.

Rotation in and out of the line had also begun. A fresh unit would relieve a tired one. The relieved men would be sent back out of range of the guns to some peaceful village, there to enjoy an idyll while their comrades on the front were mired in squalor. Up front, the trenches were often knee-deep in mud. Red slugs crawled the walls and frogs splashed on the floor. Rats and roaches were everywhere. Each day Tommies and *poilus* searched their shirts for "seam squirrels." They went regularly through delousing stations in the rear. While they bathed, their clothes were cleaned in a steam chamber. But a day after their return to the front, they were once more infested with lice.

Alan Seeger, the young American poet who fought with the British, made entries in his diary descriptive of this dual life. One day he wrote: "Every minute here is worth weeks of ordinary experience. This will spoil one for any other kind of life." A few days later it was: "We are not leading the life of men at all, but that of animals, living in holes in the ground, and only showing outside to fight and to feed."

Now, as autumn neared, General Joffre made it clear that the lesson he had learned from Artois was indeed nothing beyond more artillery and men and a still wider front. General Pétain was to hurl about half a million men at the German positions in Champagne, about the middle of the western front. Above him, Sir Douglas Haig was to lead the British out of Artois again.

This, the greatest of Joffre's attempts to burst through the German line, began on September 22, 1915. It opened with the roaring of nine hundred heavy and sixteen hundred light guns. They thundered on for three days.

"Your *élan* will be irresistible!" Joffre told his troops, and the French advanced with bands playing the *Marseillaise*. It looked like a walk-through again, but it was another stroll into hell. The Germans had merely pulled back to sit out the artillery barrage. After the French had cut through the first line of trenches, even the second and third, their *élan* flagged. It was then that the Germans struck.

The Champagne offensive raged for ten days, and it ended after the Allies ran out of shells. No less than 4,967,000 rounds had been fired, enough to supply a war the size of Korea. And France had lost another 145,000 men.

Up in the north, Sir Douglas Haig fared no better. The British were also thwarted, and 60,000 men were cut down. Germany's losses all along the line were 178,000 men. Thus, in a single battle, there were over 200,000 casualties. As a result of this dreadful waste of humanity Field Marshal Sir John French was relieved of his command, and Sir Douglas Haig was installed as commander of the British Expeditionary Force. However, this meant only that one brass hat had been replaced by another equally unable to understand the changed nature of war.

The year 1915 had ended in a bloody, baffling deadlock.

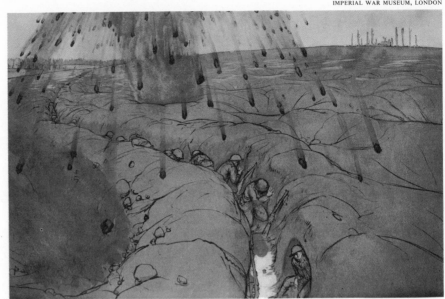

Scenes on these pages show various aspects of trench warfare on the western front in 1915. Below, a small contingent of British soldiers is photographed leaving the trenches on one of the frequent small raids that filled the gaps between major battles. The drawing at right by a Briton, H. S. Williamson, captures the tension in British ranks as shells explode above their trenches. At left, German soldiers battle it out with the enemy.

Self-reliant poilus *like this fellow were the heroes of Verdun.*

THEY SHALL NOT PASS!

6

Upon the arrival of winter the Allies believed that they would have a six-month respite in which to rest and regroup. However, General Falkenhayn had spent his Christmas holidays brooding over the situation.

Germany, he reported to the Kaiser, could not win a drawn-out war. Her manpower reserves were too thin. The war had to be won right away, and this by breaking the will of France. If France were to be bled white, she would collapse and England would withdraw from the Continent.

Moreover, France must be dealt a psychological blow. Some place sacred to her must be captured. Verdun was the very place. Here was the city once burned by Attila the Hun. Here was the place where the heirs of Charlemagne divided the Frankish empire. Here, in the center of the western front, was the Allied bulge menacing the Germans. And here, finally, was the Citadel of France. If Verdun fell, all France would go into mourning.

General Falkenhayn did not want Verdun to fall too quickly. He wanted to create rivers of blood and keep them flowing. He deliberately shortened his front. He kept his reserves well away from the battle commander. On a limited front, he could not achieve a breakthrough. If one were to happen by chance, the reserves would be too far away to pour through the gap. This was a diabolical plan, for Falkenhayn's object was to get as many people killed as possible.

Beginning in January, 1916, the Germans moved with incredible speed to get their troops and guns in position. Five railways were built especially to do the job. They hauled about one thousand light and heavy guns to the front. Among them were thirteen of the Big Berthas, plus giant mine throwers, naval rifles, and gas-discharging tubes. Three million shells were stockpiled to keep the guns bellowing for three days, and a force of perhaps half a million men was assembled.

All this was done under the nose of the French. General Joffre and the French High Command still thought that if any major push was coming, it would occur in the north in Flanders. They believed that the Allies possessed a safe superiority of 132 divisions to 100 for the Germans. The reason they thought Verdun secure was that the German build-up was on such a narrow front. It was only along the east bank of the river Meuse, which splits Ver-

Erich von Falkenhayn planned the German drive on Verdun.

HISTORISCHES BILDARCHIV HANDKE, BAD BERNECK

dun in two. If it had been on both banks, the French would have been truly alarmed. They would have feared an attempt to break through. They could not possibly have guessed Falkenhayn's dark design.

Verdun, meanwhile, had been reduced by the necessities of war to the shadow of a citadel. It was still composed of twenty forts and forty redoubts formed in a fortress ring. But most of the guns had been shipped to other sectors. Only a few thousand slothful garrison troops manned the outer defenses.

Fortunately for France, fogs along the Meuse delayed the attack. In that interval, reports of growing German strength induced Joffre to send a few divisions toward the city. Then the assault began.

On February 21, the German guns began roaring in an attempt to create a "zone of death" before Verdun. Some two million shells were poured on a six-mile front. They were a devilish mixture of shrapnel, high explosive, and poison gas blanketing the area between the forts. The monster projectiles hurled by the Big Berthas were reserved for use against the fortifications.

At dusk of the first day the bombardment subsided. Scouts came forward. They were to test the French defenses. They did not expect to find any survivors. To their amazement, they were shot at!

Singed and blackened scarecrows in the French outposts opened up a crackling rifle fire. The German scouts withdrew, and the bombardment was resumed with redoubled fury in the morning.

It was then that the battle was joined. The Germans came on in gray waves about a hundred yards apart. Pioneers and grenadiers came first, to clear barbed wire or remaining obstacles. Then came the main body in single file. Next were the reserves, bringing up ammunition, tools, and sandbags. Sometimes the reserves were fed into the fighting lines. On and on they came, the second line passing through or reinforcing the first line, and so on—grim, gray leapfroggers following the billowing smoke, sliding through the ravines, taking cover in the forests, cutting off and reducing the French strong points one by one. Always the bombardment moved in front of them. Trenches collapsed. Pillboxes were shattered. Forts were shredded. And inside all of them lay crushed or bleeding Frenchmen.

By the night of February 24, Verdun was tottering. If General Falkenhayn had released his reserves then, the citadel city might have fallen. But he did not, according to plan. Even so, next day German storm troops took Fort Douaumont. Everywhere, the French were falling back. On that same day,

The German infantry assault on Verdun was preceded by a two-day artillery bombardment. In the historic photograph below left, a 38-cm. German gun fires the first shot at Fort Douaumont, a prime military target. At right, two aerial photographs—an innovation at Verdun—show the gradual reduction of the once formidable fort to pockmocked mire. Only the polygonal outlines remain to testify to its former existence. After this barrage the Germans expected to march unopposed over a wasteland of seared timber and mutilated bodies. They did not include in their reckoning the French will to resist.

General Pétain (standing, center) was called upon to reorganize the severely battered French divisions at Verdun.

General Joffre ordered Henri Philippe Pétain to save Verdun.

That night, General Pétain called General Balfourier, commander of the key eastern sector, and said: "General Pétain speaking. I am taking over. Inform your troops. Keep up your courage. I know I can depend on you."

"Very well, sir, we shall bear up," Balfourier replied. "You can rely on us, as we rely on you."

Thus, in the storybook style of which the French are so fond, began the heroic defense of Verdun. Throughout that night and into the early morning, General Pétain and his chief of staff prepared the French stand. Pétain stood before a map pasted on the wall of the Town Hall in Souilly. Seizing a piece of charcoal, he sketched the sectors already lost to the Germans. Then he marked where they would strike next, dictating the orders that were delivered to the holding forces that sunup.

From that night on the French turned and fought their tormentors. There were now as many as a million men locked in battle. Back and forth it went, a dreadful seesaw in which each advance or retreat meant the lives of thousands of men. Meanwhile, General Pétain decided he had to organize his weak

communications lines into a more adequate system.

To supply half a million men and 150,000 draft animals was a task too huge to be handled by the one existing branch line and a narrow-gauge railway. Pétain ordered the rebuilding of the road to Bar-le-Duc in the rear. It was to be called *La Voie Sacrée*—the Sacred Way—and over it came 3,000 trucks rushing supplies to the front, rumbling back for more, then rushing up again. It was like a conveyer belt, and it was the first time in the history of warfare that motor transport was used to supply a fighting front.

Gradually, Verdun stiffened. By appealing to the soul of France on one hand, and putting his engineers to work on the other, Pétain had formed an invincible weapon. Shaken, General Falkenhayn began to realize that Verdun might not collapse. He broadened his front, extending it to the west. He was too late. The Germans collided with fresh French divisions, which had come rolling up the Sacred Way. The Germans recoiled. They came again in floods of field gray, and a blood-drenched battle raged over a scabrous hill named the Dead Man. Throughout March it raged, and the French held. On April 9, the fiercest German thrust of all rolled against the Dead Man and then slid down it in defeat.

By the middle of the month it was the French who were attacking. Verdun had held, but the dreadful battle was to rage onward through December, when Fort Douaumont was at last retaken.

No battle in history has ever been more costly or more fruitless. France lost half a million men killed, wounded, or captured. Germany lost four hundred thousand. Falkenhayn's rivers of blood had indeed flowed, but the fortress city did not fall. Instead, the spirit of France had rallied magnificently to a memorable cry—"*Ils ne passeront pas!*" (they shall not pass). Rather than being crushed, France was now up and fighting.

And now it was the turn of the Allied High Command to try to break the long-drawn-out deadlock on the western front.

It has been said that the Battle of the Somme was fought by the British to draw the Germans away from Verdun. This is not true. At the end of 1915,

There was little change on the western front in 1916. Small gains were made by the Germans at Verdun (black arrows) and the Allies (white arrows) at the Somme. The inset shows the progress of the Somme offensive, begun on July 1 (broken black line).

before the Germans struck at Verdun, General Joffre had proposed to General Haig that a great battle be fought at the Somme as soon as good weather appeared.

Haig was for a big battle, but in Flanders on the far left flank. Nevertheless, he came to agree with Joffre. Both commanders still believed that massive concentrations of men and guns at a single point would break the deadlock. Sir Douglas Haig even believed that he might split the Germans in two in a single day. He would attack on both sides of the Somme River, which runs between Artois in the north and Picardy in the south. On the north side of the river Sir Douglas placed fourteen British divisions, and on the south side were five French divisions. More than one thousand guns were mounted to crush the Germans. Sir Douglas had his Cavalry Corps saddled and bridled to go galloping across no man's land "into the blue."

By late April it became plain to the Germans in the Somme that the British were organizing their Big Push. The German commander informed General Falkenhayn. The Chief of Staff replied that it would be too good to be true. His own army was then being mangled at Verdun and he could not believe that the Allies would be as stupid as he had been. Moreover, the German defenses at the Somme had been transformed into a concrete honeycomb.

Still, the Big Push was coming, and it would lead to the introduction of the war's most important secret weapon. Once again, Winston Churchill must be credited for a major innovation. While at the Admiralty he had allowed funds to be diverted for the development of a "land battleship." Thus the tank was born. It got its strange name because of the secrecy surrounding its birth. People who inquired what this strange new mechanical monster might be were told that it was a "water carrier." But because the initials "W. C." are identical with those of the British water closet, or toilet, the name was changed to tank.

Unfortunately, General Haig was too hasty in using this new weapon, which was to revolutionize warfare. Instead of waiting until a large force of tanks could be assembled and so burst upon the enemy in demoralizing droves, he started the battle

A prototype of the tank introduced at the Somme is shown undergoing a tryout in England in January, 1916.

A German skeleton (right) lies unburied on a muddy battlefield at the Somme, many months after the bloodiest slaughter of the war. Casualties for both sides ran over one million. "Hell cannot be so terrible," wrote a French lieutenant in his diary.

without them. Three months later, he grabbed the first forty-two tanks to come off the assembly line and hurled them into the general melee. They scared the German soldiers out of their wits—as they still scare all soldiers—but there were not enough of them to change the battle.

By then the Battle of the Somme was only a second blood bath to rival the carnage of Verdun. Sir Douglas Haig should have called it off after the first day, by which time he had already lost sixty thousand men. But Joffre urged him to continue. Like Joffre, Haig was a man who thought of troops as digits. He kept feeding them into the meat grinder in six figures. The Battle of the Somme ended on November 18. Each side had lost six hundred thousand men in this most somber battle in the annals of British arms.

At the Somme, cavalry charged for one of the last times in a major engagement, and tanks rolled for the first. Otherwise it was a military cipher.

But 1916—the year of the great bloodletting—did produce powerful repercussions in the Allied capitals. Lloyd George became the British Prime Minister, and Georges Clemenceau moved a step closer to the premiership of France. Papa Joffre was given a marshal's baton, but command of the French ar-

mies passed to General Robert Nivelle, one of the heroes of Verdun. Sir Douglas Haig was also made a field marshal, although he remained in command.

In Russia, the Czar gained a temporary stay of his doom through the June offensive launched by the capable General Aleksei Brusilov. The Brusilov Offensive nearly punched through the Carpathian passes into Austria. The fighting cost Germany and Austria six hundred thousand men, no less than four hundred thousand Austrians falling captive. But the Brusilov Offensive also tore apart more strands in the Czarist fabric. One million Russians were lost. The Czarist army was no longer a military force but a seedbed for revolution.

That same year Emperor Francis Joseph of Austria died. His great-nephew, the son of the murdered Archduke's brother, came to the throne. Emperor Charles longed to break the German hold on his army. His foreign minister yearned for peace. The empire that had begun the war—unaware that it had also prepared its own demise—now hungered to end it. Finally, General Conrad stepped down as Chief of Staff. He was the last of the high commanders who had been in on the beginning.

Erich von Falkenhayn's hold on his position as the successor to Moltke steadily weakened. A snub

CONTINUED ON PAGE 69

Shouting defiance, bayonets raised, French soldiers charge into battle in this painting, called The Assault. *It was General Nivelle who coined for his soldiers the famous boast of resistance: "They shall not pass!" That motto rallied France in a moment of grave peril. After the French had halted the German drive at Verdun, it became the watchcry for the nation.*

MUSEE DE LA GUERRE, PARIS

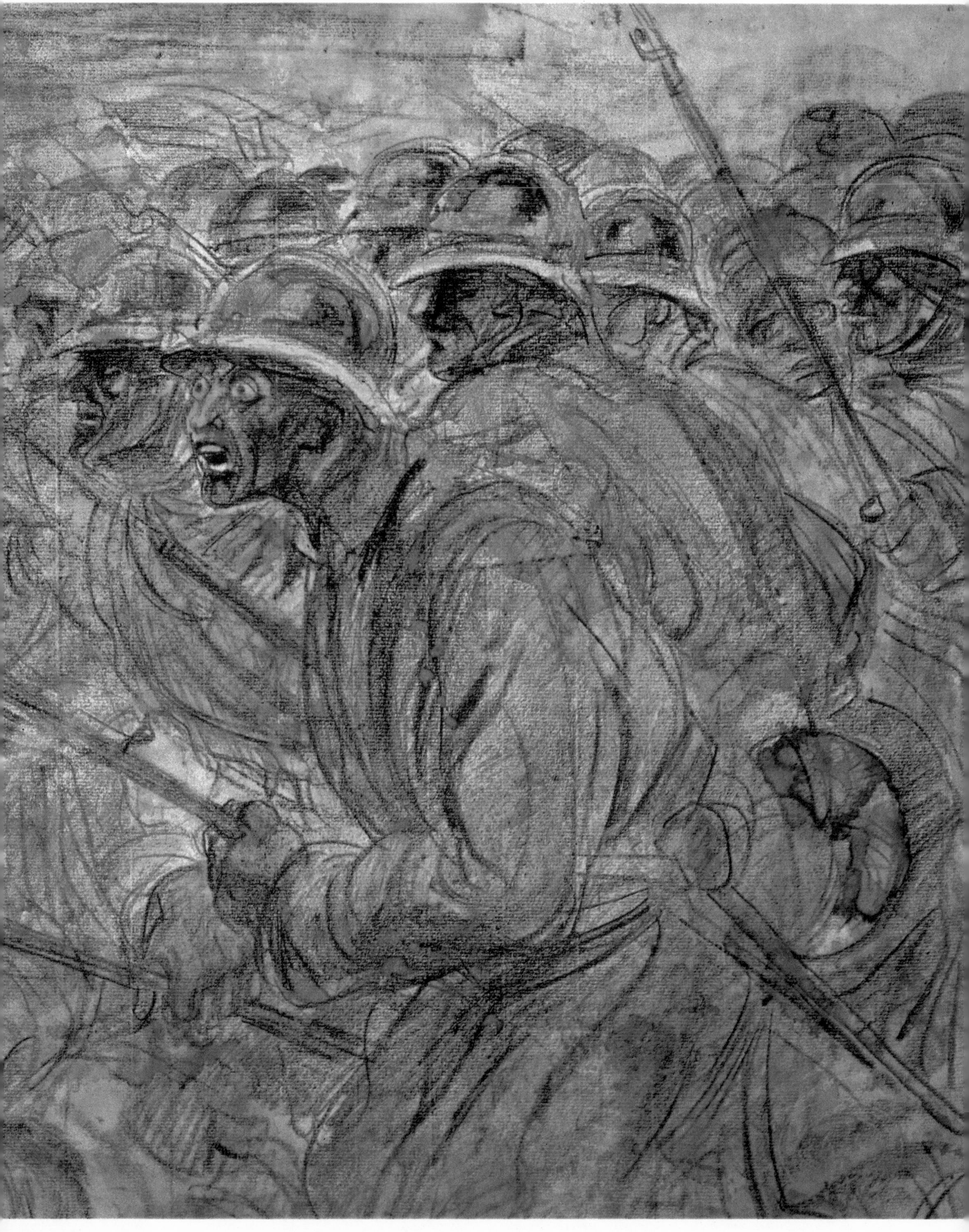

ALL: IMPERIAL WAR MUSEUM, LONDON

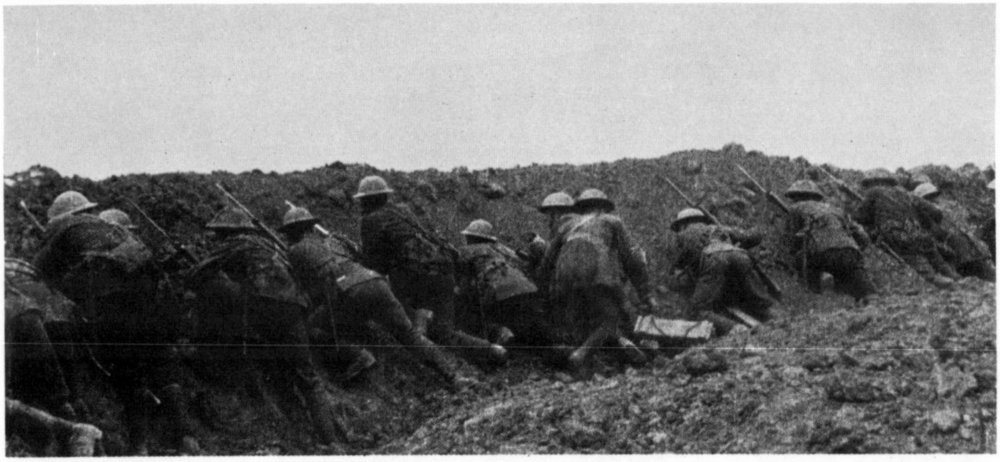

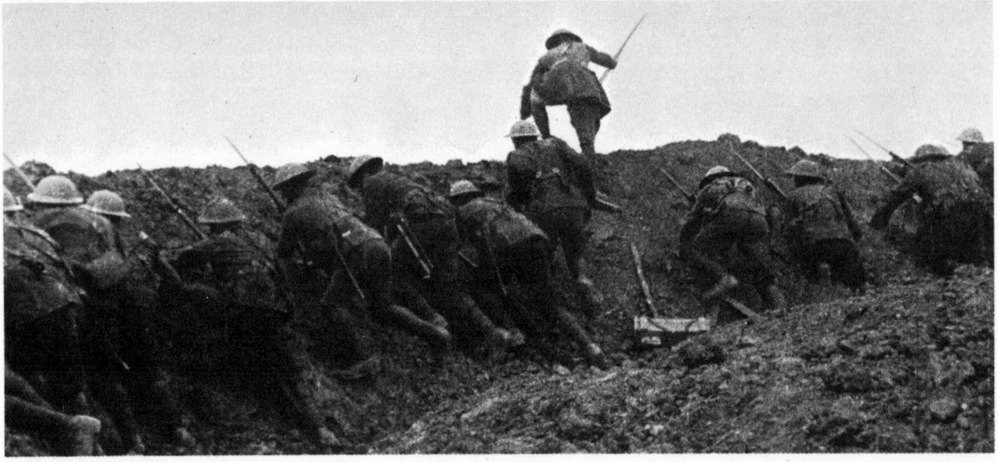

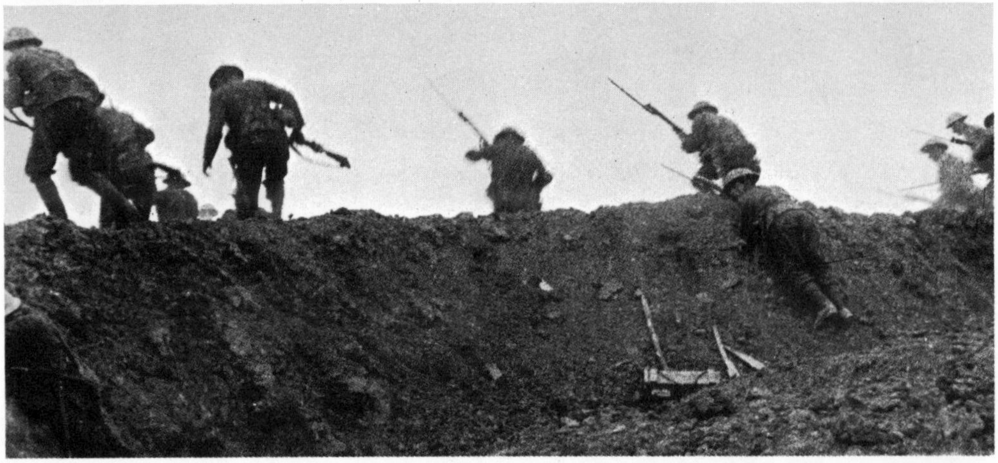

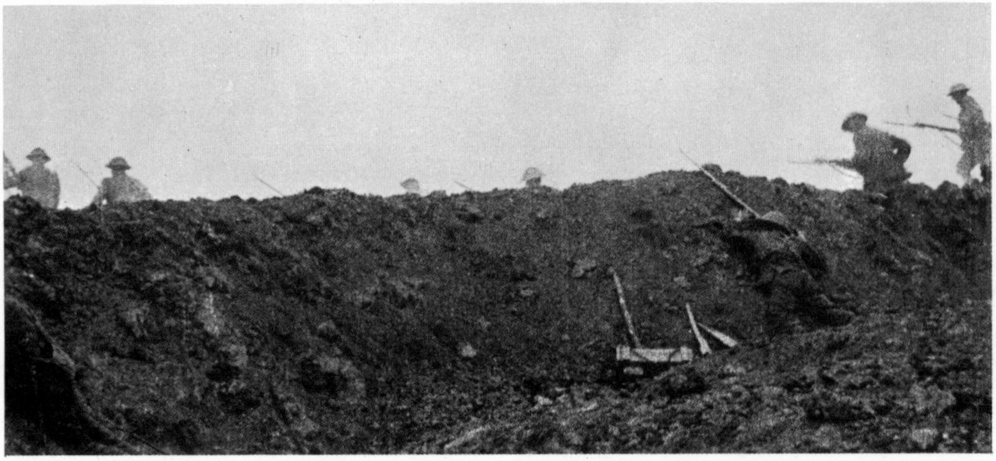

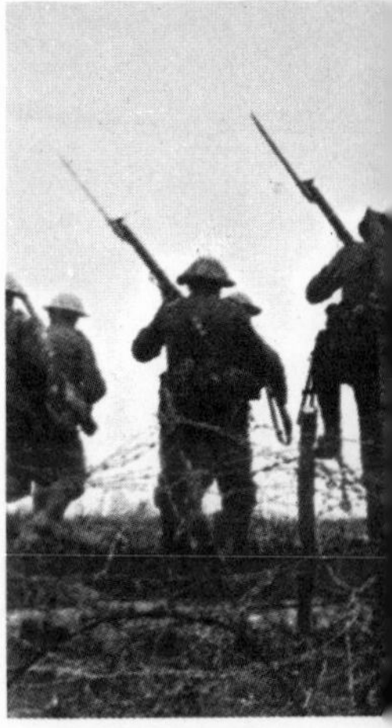

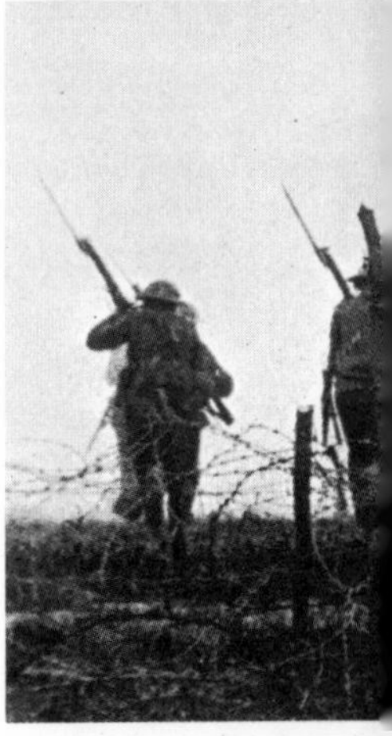

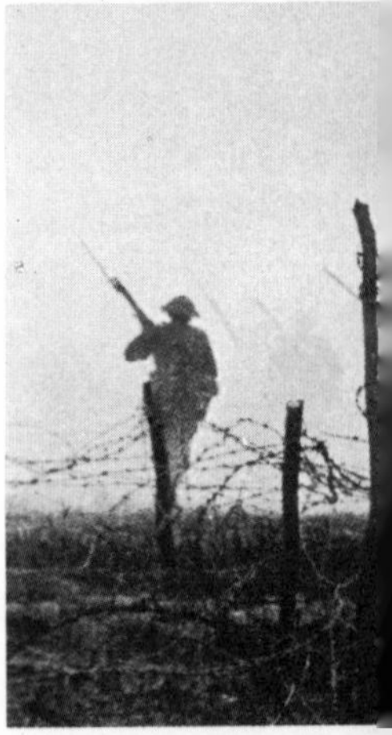

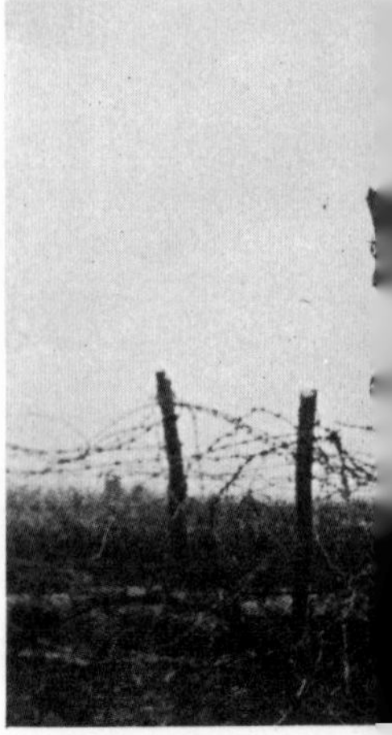

from the Kaiser on his conduct of the war made it plain that his resignation was desired. He handed it in, and Hindenburg and Ludendorff moved west to occupy his headquarters and run the entire war. Eventually, they would run the empire—or at least Ludendorff would. Through Hindenburg, his superior—but actually his mouthpiece—Ludendorff would dictate even to the Kaiser.

Yet General Falkenhayn, demoted to a field command on the eastern front, helped destroy the Rumanian Army in late 1916. Rumania, watching which way to jump, had been misled by the successes of the Brusilov Offensive. She declared war on Austria on August 27, 1916. The Germans, who had expected this move, were ready. They moved rapidly against Rumania. By mid-December they had captured more than two thirds of the country, including the capital, Bucharest, and scooped up all but a few remnants of the Rumanian Army into their prison cages.

So the snows of yet another winter muffled both fronts in white silence. They fell again on sprawling corpses and shaped them softly into mounds.

This winter there were more of them than usual.

Eight fast sequence photographs from motion pictures record the front line drama of the Somme advance. From top to bottom far left, men are shown crouching in the trenches in readiness and then emerging following an officer. In the third photo one soldier is hit and slips back into the empty trench. In the next sequence, the advancing cameraman photographs the progress of the troops through the barbed wire: two men are hit by German gunfire. In the remaining two photographs a lone soldier hurries to join his companions who have pushed ahead and disappeared into smoke and fog.

The power of the British Navy is conveyed by Philip Connard in his painting of the Harwich Force maneuvering at sea. As war began, England had the world's largest navy.

THE WAR AT SEA 7

The Allies had expected to command the waves. The French Navy was to watch the Mediterranean while the rest of the world's open water would be patrolled by the gigantic English Navy.

This meant that it was up to Britain to drive Germany from the sea.

In the beginning, the British fared poorly. The German cruisers *Goeben* and *Breslau* were allowed to make their momentous voyage to Turkey and the Black Sea. In that same first month of the war, the English retaliated. Vice-Admiral Sir David Beatty led his flotilla of battle cruisers into the Heligoland Bight on Germany's North Sea coast. They sailed right into Germany's front yard and sank the light cruisers *Köln*, *Mainz*, and *Ariadne*, in addition to one destroyer.

Fortune changed sides again in September. A German U-boat put a torpedo into the British cruiser *Aboukir* off the Dutch coast, and then sank both the *Hogue* and the *Cressy* with nearly all hands. In October, the battleship *Audacious* hit a German mine off Ireland and plunged to the bottom.

The sea war then shifted to the Pacific. Admiral Count Maximilian von Spee led Germany's Far East Squadron to a point off the coast of Chile in South America. His purpose was to prey on Allied shipping there. Informed of Spee's whereabouts, the British Admiralty ordered Admiral Sir Christopher Cradock to search for Spee's raiders and bring them to battle. It was not an order but a death notice. Cradock's cruisers *Good Hope* and *Monmouth*, and the light cruiser *Glasgow*, were no match for the powerful *Scharnhorst* and *Gneisenau*. Still, the admiral obeyed orders.

On November 1, he came upon Spee's flotilla off the Chilean coast. A terrible night battle ensued. Great spiky naval cannon probed the night sky and tongues of flame leaped from their mouths. Projectiles streaked across the ocean like huge fleeing blobs of red. Stricken ships bucked and whipsawed, and the sound of huge explosions went rolling like thunder across glistening black waves. Sometimes plumes of water rose majestically into the sky to become illumined with the glare of battle, melting back into the dark sea like slowly vanishing flames.

When it was over, the *Good Hope* and the *Monmouth* were on the bottom and Admiral Cradock and most of his men were dead.

Now Admiral Spee was free to attack Allied shipping in the Pacific, and an alarmed Admiralty sent the battle cruisers *Inflexible* and *Invincible* rushing to the rescue. Vice-Admiral Sir F. Doveton Sturdee commanded this force. He made for the British base at Port Stanley in the Falkland Islands off Argentina's Atlantic coast. On schedule, he sailed into the port to fill his empty bunkers with coal; then he would sail out again, steer south, and swing around Cape Horn into the Pacific and begin hunting for Spee.

But on December 1, Spee was heading north. He brought his fleet around the Horn into the Atlantic and prepared to bombard Port Stanley. Too late he saw the British sluggers inside, and turned to flee. The *Inflexible* and the *Invincible* fired their boilers and sped after him. Firing at their leisure at long range they sent the *Scharnhorst* and the *Gneisenau* to the bottom and later picked off the little cruisers *Nürnberg* and *Leipzig*. The *Dresden* escaped only to be sunk the following March at about the point where Cradock had met disaster.

The victory in the Battle of the Falklands restored Britain's prestige as Queen of the Waves. Her status rose even higher when news came of what had happened to the German commercial raider *Emden*.

This light cruiser commanded by Captain Karl von Müller was the scourge of the Indian Ocean. From August to November she captured thirteen ships. The very sea lanes from India to Britain were imperiled. Open sea lanes, of course, are the purpose of sea power. The many raw materials and manufactured goods that industrial nations require to conduct a war can only be transported by sea; unchallenged sea lanes are also needed so that troops can be moved quickly from one theatre of war to another. But in the Indian Ocean, Captain Müller's cruiser was paralyzing this vital traffic. Moreover, he and his men often put in to Indian ports to spread propaganda against the Allies. But Captain Müller was as gallant as a knight. He treated his prisoners kindly, observed international law, and never opened fire on illegitimate targets.

Müller's spectacular career came to an end before 1914 was over. The heavier, stronger Australian cruiser *Sydney* came up with the *Emden* off the Cocos Islands. A slugging match began and ended with the blazing *Emden* being driven onto a reef. Because of his great gallantry, Müller and his officers were allowed to carry their swords into captivity.

Britain continued victorious at sea into 1915. In January of that year, Admiral Beatty engaged a smaller German squadron sixty miles off the English coast. In this encounter that was called the Battle of the Dogger Bank, Germany lost the *Blücher* and 951 men, while British losses were only fourteen men killed and six wounded.

By this time, England's immense sea power had begun to tell against Germany: her blockade had reduced the flow of munitions to Germany from neutral countries to a trickle. Enraged, Germany announced that she would consider all grain and flour as the contraband of war. Contraband, of course, is prohibited goods. There are two kinds: equipment for war; and foodstuffs for armies. Britain had prevented very much of the first from reaching Germany. Now, in retaliation, Germany was declaring that certain foods—whether meant for troops or civilians—were contraband. And she recognized that to back up her words with destructive power she would need submarines, in large numbers.

Britain then used Germany's contraband policy as an excuse to seize a neutral ship docked at Falmouth with a food cargo bound for Germany. The Kaiser announced in blind fury that henceforth all goods moving toward Britain were contraband. After February 18, 1915, he said, the waters around England were to be considered a combat zone. Enemy merchant ships found within them "would

be destroyed without it always being possible to warn the crews and passengers." Clearly, what the German warriors had in mind was submarine warfare of the most brutal sort.

Britain reacted by proclaiming a counter blockade. From now on no neutral ship would be allowed to enter or leave a German port, no matter what it carried. From that decision stemmed the starvation of the German people. It was not so much that the importation of foodstuffs fell off, it was that chemical fertilizers could not get into the country. German plants could not make up this loss, because the nitrates were needed for the manufacture of munitions. So the soil grew weaker and weaker and what was grown was less nourishing.

Rationing and belt tightening began in 1915. By 1917, however, famine stalked the German land. Its chief victims were the poor, the sickly, the aged, and the children. It has been claimed that 750,000 Germans starved to death because of the blockade. Such a figure can never be proved. But even if it were cut in half, it would still be about fifty times greater than the number of persons who lost their lives on Allied ships as the result of Germany's submarine warfare.

Yet, because the submarine attacks were so spectacular and so sudden—like a snake striking without warning—they drew the world's immediate attention and its outrage. Moreover, it was stupid of the Kaiser to have turned his U-boats loose. Britain had already angered all the neutrals—including the United States—by her absolute blockade. Germany should have tried to take advantage of that. Instead, she was to offend the most powerful neutral of all, the United States of America.

The great duel for control of the seas was fought between England and Germany with the assistance of their allies. Encounters in the Atlantic, at the Falkland Islands, and in the Indian Ocean demonstrated the global scope of naval warfare. In the photograph at top right, three Russian ships engage the Turkish-owned, German-manned cruiser Goeben *in the Bosporus. Ships of the German fleet (center) execute intricate maneuvers prior to facing the British at Jutland. Sailors on the German ship* Blücher *(bottom right), a victim of British fire at Dogger Bank, jump to safety as the ship keels over.*

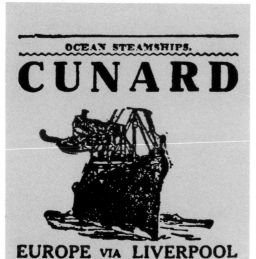

OCEAN STEAMSHIPS.
CUNARD

EUROPE VIA LIVERPOOL
LUSITANIA

Fastest and Largest Steamer
now in Atlantic Service Sails
SATURDAY, MAY 1, 10 A. M.
Transylvania, Fri., May 7, 5 P.M.
Orduna, - - Tues., May 18, 10 A.M.
Tuscania, - - Fri., May 21, 5 P.M.
LUSITANIA, Sat., May 29, 10 A.M.
Transylvania, Fri., June 4, 5 P.M.

Gibraltar—Genoa—Naples—Piraeus
S.S. Carpathia, Thur., May 13, Noon

NOTICE!

TRAVELLERS intending to
embark on the Atlantic voyage
are reminded that a state of
war exists between Germany
and her allies and Great Britain
and her allies; that the zone of
war includes the waters adja-
cent to the British Isles; that,
in accordance with formal notice given by the Imperial German Government, vessels flying
the flag of Great Britain, or of
any of her allies, are liable to
destruction in those waters and
that travellers sailing in the
war zone on ships of Great
Britain or her allies do so at
their own risk.

IMPERIAL GERMAN EMBASSY

WASHINGTON, D. C., APRIL 22, 1915.

The Lusitania, *pride of the Cunard line,
sails out of New York harbor (below) bound
for Liverpool. On the day of her departure,
May 1, 1915, a notice (left) appeared
warning passengers of wartime conditions
existing in the waters surrounding the British Isles. To the excitement of a trans-At-
lantic crossing was added the suspense of
possible danger. It was an uneventful voyage
until on May 7, in sight of Ireland, disaster
struck. A German U-boat sent two torpedoes
crashing through the ship's hull. The Lusitania sank in 18 minutes, and 1,198 perished.*

74

It was in late April, 1915, that the splendid British liner, the *Lusitania*, prepared to sail from New York to Liverpool. The German Government had already published a warning that such ships would be sunk on sight. But only one passenger canceled passage, and on May 1 the stately ship cast off and made for the open sea.

On May 7, Commander Walter Schwieger of the submarine *U-20* watched the *Lusitania*'s progress through his periscope. He ordered two torpedoes sent flashing toward her. Eighteen minutes after the first one hit, the *Lusitania* was on the bottom. With her went 1,198 persons, most of them civilians. Among these were 128 American citizens, most of them women and children.

America rocked with rage. The nation had once been pro-British in sympathy but firmly neutral in attitude. Pro-German groups had been permitted to function (see overleaf). Now, everything German was despised, and it was a rash voice indeed that was lifted in the Kaiser's defense. Not even the invasion of Belgium surpasses the *Lusitania* sinking as a German blunder.

"Only to these two grand crimes and blunders of history," Winston Churchill wrote, "were her undoing and our salvation due."

Still, America did not move. President Wilson said: "There is such a thing as a man being too proud to fight." As the President would discover, not too many Americans agreed with that remark.

In late May, the British Grand Fleet put to sea to sweep the English coasts of gathering flocks of German submarines. At about the same time the German High Seas Fleet risked the open sea and began steaming toward the Skagerrak, the waterway separating Norway from Denmark.

Admiral Sir John Jellicoe commanded the Grand Fleet. He had 28 battleships, 9 battle cruisers, 8 armored cruisers, 26 light cruisers, and 78 destroyers.

Admiral Reinhard Scheer commanded the High Seas Fleet. He had 22 battleships, 5 battle cruisers,

President Wilson advertises his candidacy on the truck above with the slogan "Peace with Honor." The hope of the President was to keep America neutral. Women pacifists (below) dramatize their attitude with fans.

11 light cruisers, and 61 destroyers and smaller ships.

Britain obviously enjoyed the advantage, 149 ships to 99. Moreover, Jellicoe had more heavies and more big guns than Scheer had.

The two fleets plowed on, unaware that they were on a collision course. The point of impact was to be off the coast of Denmark's Jutland Peninsula. It was this promontory that gave its name to what became the greatest naval battle of World War I.

On the afternoon of May 31, Admiral Jellicoe heard from Admiral Beatty, commanding the battle cruisers. "We see a large amount of smoke as from a fleet bearing E.N.E."

Jellicoe ordered him to steam for the smoke. Beatty did and brought his nine battle cruisers in on the five German ships of similar rank com-

Above, President Wilson delivers a speech during his 1916 campaign for re-election.

San Francisco's German-Americans established a German Relief Fund. Each nail in this 1915 "Iron Cross" marked a gift.

77

During World War I battleships grew bigger and better, thanks to superior firepower and to shipyards' increasing ability to work with steel. Below, a painting shows a clumsy Austrian monitor in action on the Danube, a craft little improved from those of the Civil War years. At right is a lithograph of a giant-sized American battleship, with radio masts and double-tiered gun turrets.

manded by Admiral Franz von Hipper. Beatty fired first, from a range of ten miles. Hipper roared back, and the battle was joined.

Within a half hour the Germans took a dreadful toll. Led by the magnificent *Derfflinger*—one of the finest shooting ships afloat—they sank the *Indefatigable* with all but two of her sailors lost. The *Queen Mary* blew up and vanished with 1,266 men. And Admiral Beatty felt his flagship *Lion* shudder under the impact of four shells from the *Lutzow*. Beatty was himself unruffled. "Chatfield," he said to his flag captain, "there seems to be something wrong with our blasted ships today. Turn two points to port."

Two points to port was nearer the enemy, and the Germans turned away! Beatty then swung back toward Jellicoe and the rest of the Grand Fleet, and the Germans pursued. Their plan had been to lure Beatty into the massed guns of the High Seas Fleet, but now it was Beatty who was luring them into those of the Grand Fleet. Battle—part melee, part running fight—was renewed. The Germans sank the armored cruiser *Defence* and dealt death blows to her sister ship, the *Warrior*. In turn, the British mortally wounded the *Lutzow*.

Still the German column came on, unsuspecting. Admiral Scheer deployed his ships in line-ahead, that is, in a long single column. At 6:16 P.M. Scheer perceived in dismay the great array of Dreadnoughts under Jellicoe.

The British had completed the basic naval maneuver called crossing the T.

Jellicoe's line lay across the approach of Scheer's column like the crosspiece in the letter T. The English could train all their guns broadside on the advancing Germans, who could fire only their forward turrets. Any attempt of the Germans to turn away would seem destined to disaster. Ships turning in succession would each try to make their turn at the same point, as though swinging around a buoy. As each one did, the massed and massive firepower of the British fleet could come converging into it. That was the dreadful situation facing Admiral Scheer, and he met it with a maneuver that had been planned to meet just such an occasion.

The High Seas Fleet turned away together! At 6:35 P.M. Scheer gave the order to "turn away to-

gether" to starboard. As one ship, that entire long column reversed its course. The first ship became the last and the last was the first. By that maneuver the German fleet saved itself. It vanished from the sight of Jellicoe's ships.

And then it reappeared! Why the Germans came back to join the issue with a larger force has never been made clear, but it is known that bedlam resulted. It was ship to ship, shell for shell. The *Black Prince* and the *Invincible* were sunk, and the *Warspite* was put out of action. The *Frauenlob* and the *Elbing* were lost, the *Pommern* was cut in two, and the *Derfflinger* and *Seydlitz* were set on fire.

It was at that point that Admiral Jellicoe with his superior force might have moved in for the kill. Some of the maimed or blazing German ships were like three-legged foxes trying to elude the hounds. But the British admiral withdrew.

Jutland, World War I's most important engagement on the high seas, gave little comfort to either side. Britain lost 117,025 tons of warships, Germany lost 61,180 tons. Tactically, Jutland was a German victory: she had given more than she got. Strategically, it was a British triumph: the High Seas Fleet returned to port and never came out again. From Jutland onward, the surface of the sea was ruled by the Queen of the Waves.

But beneath the sea, the new German challenge was threatening to drag the British Navy under.

Germany's sink-on-sight U-boat warfare had always been a matter for heated debate in the highest councils of the nation. Navy Minister Admiral Alfred von Tirpitz was for it. He saw with merciless clarity that Germany's navy was not big enough to wrest supremacy of the sea from Britain. However, the submarine, a relatively new weapon, might be used to gnaw on the British life lines and cut them in two. Merchant ships were helpless against these undersea wolves. Admiral Tirpitz insisted that the submarine warfare was the only chance Germany had to humble the proud might of the British Navy.

Chancellor Theobald von Bethmann-Holweg argued against this proposal, especially after he felt the whip of American anger following the sinking of the *Lusitania*. Bethmann wanted to abandon U-

This remarkable photograph of an English submarine being strafed was taken from a German airplane.

boat warfare rather than turn the world against Germany. For months the Kaiser veered between these two views, while an exchange of diplomatic notes took place. Finally, frightened by the prospect of America entering the war against him, the Kaiser agreed with Bethmann. The U-boat warfare was called off in late 1916. But only temporarily.

General Ludendorff echoed Tirpitz's argument. He arrogantly beat down all of Bethmann's protests. Victory was worth any price, he said. On January 9, 1917, a message went from the Kaiser to all his ships:

"I order that unrestricted submarine warfare be launched with the greatest vigor on February 1. You will immediately take the necessary steps."

Thus was begun the ordeal of the world's merchant seamen. Day after day, night after night, lookouts aboard slow-moving freighters and tankers would strain their eyes for the dreadful sight of telltale bubbles heading for their vessels. Seeing them, they would shout a warning. If it came early enough, the ship's master might be able to maneuver his vessel out of the way. If it was too late, there was a shudder and a roar as the lethal "fish" rammed

through the ship's side to explode within—and another victim of Ludendorff's mad policy would sink beneath the waves.

By the end of February there were an appalling number of such victims. In that month alone, 781,500 tons of Allied shipping had been lost. Britain was shaken as she had not been since the days of Napoleon.

At the start of the war the Allies possessed 21,000,000 tons of shipping. This was about 6,000,000 tons more than was needed to feed England and supply the Allied armies. But in a two-month period, Allied shipping losses totaled 2,100,000 tons. One third of the surplus was gone already. Because shipyards were far from able to replace such staggering losses, and because Germany was putting more and more submarines into the battle, the surplus might quickly disappear. After that, if inroads were made on the necessary 15,000,000 tons, the Allied position might become impossible.

Clearly, unchecked German U-boat warfare could doom the Allied cause.

SÜDDEUTSCHER VERLAG, MUNICH

Admiral Tirpitz (top left, full face), architect of the German U-boat campaign, confers with another admiral. Above, survivors from a torpedoed British freighter are rescued by a German submarine.

Two sketches by Francis Dodd show British submarine crewmen on duty. The man at right peers through a periscope; those above are adjusting torpedoes.

ENTER THE YANKS 8

If it was the warlike Austrian fop Count Berchtold who began World War I, then it was the equally vain and foolish German Kaiser who sealed the Central Powers' doom.

As 1917 began, the Kaiser had his chance for peace with honor. On January 22, President Wilson declared to the United States Senate that there could be "peace without victory." Kaiser Wilhelm might have begun courting the President then. He might have offered to return Alsace-Lorraine to France, thus placating the Allies. Instead, he launched the unrestricted submarine campaign.

President Wilson was so enraged that he broke off diplomatic relations with Germany. Then England informed him of the famous "Zimmermann telegram," which the German foreign minister had sent to the German ambassador in Mexico. It said:

WE INTEND TO BEGIN UNRESTRICTED SUBMARINE WARFARE. WE SHALL ENDEAVOR TO KEEP THE UNITED STATES NEUTRAL. IN THE EVENT OF THIS NOT SUCCEEDING, WE MAKE MEXICO A PROPOSAL OF ALLIANCE ON THE FOLLOWING BASIS: MAKE WAR TOGETHER, MAKE PEACE TOGETHER, GENEROUS FINANCIAL SUPPORT, AND AN UNDERSTANDING ON OUR PART THAT MEXICO IS TO RECONQUER THE LOST TERRITORY IN TEXAS, NEW MEXICO, AND ARIZONA.

There was also a proposal that if America entered the war against Germany, the President of Mexico should invite Japan to change sides and fight against the United States. It was all very silly. Mexico had no military power. She was overrun by revolutionaries and on the verge of anarchy.

Nevertheless, the Zimmermann telegram left Americans grinding their teeth and raging for war. "There is no question about going to war," former

James Montgomery Flagg painted this famous Army recruiting poster in appropriately patriotic colors. An urgent Uncle Sam points out whom he wants in the ranks of the U.S. Army.

President Theodore Roosevelt thundered. "Germany is already at war with us!" Warlike parades were staged all over the country. Marchers carried banners saying, "On to Berlin!" "Kill the Kaiser!" and "Let's Get the Hun!"

On March 16, the American ships *City of Memphis* and *Illinois* were torpedoed. And that was the end of American neutrality. On the night of April 2, the Congress convened in joint session. The Capitol was packed. The Supreme Court justices were present. They and many Congressmen wore little American flags in their lapels. There was a hush as the President began to speak.

"There is one choice we cannot make, we are incapable of making: we will not choose the path of submission." Some of the spectators were overcome with emotion, and the President continued: "The world must be made safe for democracy. Its peace must be founded on the trusted foundations of political liberty." Then President Wilson asked Congress for a declaration of war against Germany.

It came on April 6. It was a fateful date in the history of Europe and the world. America's long isolation was at an end. For the first time in her history she was crossing the Atlantic to involve herself in a war among the Great Powers.

It now remained to field an army to fight in it.

A nation of seventy million people, the United States had an army of fewer than two hundred thousand men. No tinier force could have been asked to fulfill the jubilant expectations of America's new allies. Moreover, the armament of the U.S. Army was obsolete. In its arsenal reposed not a single weapon up to European standards.

Few of the Army's top officers knew very much about the problems of high command. Lower-echelon generals were not familiar with the divisional system of organization. They were used to an army of regiments. Not too many of the Army's younger

The New York American *headlines the news of April 7 (above left). Blindfolded, the President (above right) prepares to pick a number that will make some civilian a soldier.*

officers regarded their calling as a professional occupation. They thought of it more in terms of gleaming leather, thundering hoofs, and card games in the officers' mess.

It was a rare enlisted man who had a high school diploma. A private's pay of fifteen dollars a month did not attract many ambitious men. Some of them —but not too many—had picked up some "war" experience in the overpublicized expedition against the Mexican bandit Pancho Villa. There was also a sprinkling of Marines who were veterans of "the Banana War" in Haiti. But the Marine Corps was not even a tenth of the size of the Army, and would never send more than two brigades to France.

It was this small, inexperienced, ill-equipped United States Army upon which America was to base its projected striking force of millions.

Americans, however, are not pessimists. The country fell to forming its ranks with the enthusiasm of a man going on an adventure. The first draft law was passed. It prescribed compulsory service for all able-bodied males between twenty-one and thirty-one. It called for 687,000 men, but only 516,212 were inducted during 1917. Meanwhile, plans were drawn for the vast camps and induction stations where these men could be assembled and trained. The wham of the hammer and the whine of the saw were heard across the land. America had become a vast and busy beehive thrumming with preparation for war.

Meanwhile, the man who was to command this American Expeditionary Force had already been selected.

General John J. ("Black Jack") Pershing had led the expedition against Pancho Villa. During

General John J. Pershing (below), followed by his staff and an official French welcoming committee, strides resolutely down the gangplank to begin his work in Europe. It would take a while fully to organize military manpower, but the arrival of the first small group of Americans heartened the dispirited French. During the following summer and autumn, troops were shipped abroad in ever-increasing numbers. At right, doughboys relax aboard a troopship that is carrying them to the fight.

THEY KEPT THE
SEA LANES OPEN

INVEST IN THE
VICTORY LIBERTY LOAN

FIRST IN
THE FIGHT—

ALWA
FAITHF

BE A U.S. MARIN

The duties of every American were suggested by propaganda posters. Above, a dramatic scene done by L. A. Shafer for the final Liberty Loan drive. At right, a recruiting poster for the U.S. Marine Corps, drawn by the prolific poster artist Flagg.

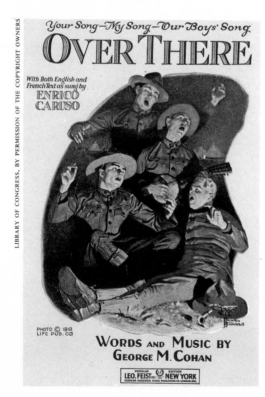

Your Song—My Song—Our Boys' Song
OVER THERE

With Both English and French Text as sung by
ENRICO CARUSO

PHOTO © 1918
LIFE PUB. CO

WORDS AND MUSIC BY
GEORGE M. COHAN

POPULAR EDITION
LEO. FEIST INC. NEW YORK
HERMAN DAREWSKI MUSIC PUBLISHING CO. LONDON, ENG.

Norman Rockwell designed the cover sheet for one of the most famous songs of the war. Tin Pan Alley kept the air full of patriotic tunes.

it, he became famous—and Americans saw many pictures of this Iron Commander who seemed every inch a soldier. Tall, strong, his flinty features adorned by a gray military mustache, Black Jack Pershing was tailor-made for monuments. He was also ambitious, a driver, and a man of very few but sharp words. He was not the sort of commander who is beloved by his troops. Indeed, there were few of those on either side in World War I. But whatever General Pershing may have lacked in warmth, he made up for with two fine personal qualities: a balanced mind and an iron will.

General Pershing began as commander of the A.E.F. by forming the 1st Infantry Division from four regular Army regiments. This would be the first American unit to go to France. Marshal Joffre had crossed the sea from France to urge immediate shipment of troops: Americans in France would be a tonic to the flagging Allies. General Pershing left before the 1st Division. On May 29, 1917, he even led an advance party of about 150 men and officers aboard the *Baltic* in New York, and sailed for England. On June 13, this group came ashore at the

The United States was so low in matériel in 1917 that recruits were forced to train with wooden guns (left). A jaunty detachment of troops (below) swings out of a New York armory on the way to boot camp. The sign outside promises "no expense" to the man who serves his country.

The enthusiasm of America's 1917 war effort is symbolized by the flag-waving Boy Scouts parading (above) along New York's Fifth Avenue in April. In the summer of that year Americans were photographed marching through the London streets (right).

French port of Boulogne on the English Channel.

The world did not yet know that the Yanks had arrived on the western front. It did, however, on the Fourth of July. On that date a battalion of picked doughboys from the 1st Division paraded in Paris. They were young and gay, they were strong, and they looked ten feet tall in their high campaign hats. As they stepped out, all the Allied high commanders knew full well that the nation these shining youths represented was wholly unprepared for war and did not even possess enough shipping to ferry its millions of raw recruits across three thousand miles of ocean. But the American soldiers were *there*, nevertheless; and as they stepped out, Paris and France took them to their hearts.

The doughboys were swept up on a sea of laughing, shouting, weeping French. They were pelted from all sides with flowers, drenched with cologne, and smeared with lipstick. "The column as it moved forward," said General Pershing, "looked like a moving flower garden."

It was impossible for the Yanks to keep order as they marched five miles from the Tomb of Napoleon to the Tomb of Lafayette. Standing beneath the statue of the great French soldier who had symbolized France's support of the American Revolution, the tight-lipped General Pershing decided to let someone else speak for him. That man was his friend, Captain Charles E. Stanton. Stepping forward, Captain Stanton saluted and cried:

"Lafayette, we are here!"

The words would go into history. At that moment, they made France delirious with joy and filled the German Kaiser with foreboding.

EXIT RUSSIA

9

Kaiser Wilhelm had two reasons for so rashly provoking the United States. One, he believed that Russia was at the breaking point. Two, he thought his submarine campaign would bring England to terms before America could influence the war.

On the first count he was right, although he should have had the patience to await the Russian collapse. On the second count he was wrong: America made her military influence felt quickly, not in France but on the sea.

Rear Admiral William S. Sims went to London three days after the United States entered the war. He conferred with Admiral Jellicoe, who was now First Sea Lord. Sims was appalled at British shipping losses.

"Looks as if the Germans are winning the war," he said.

"They will unless we stop these losses," was Admiral Jellicoe's reply.

Sims set to work to solve the problem with Vice-Admiral Sir Lewis Bayly, who was in charge of anti-submarine patrolling out of Northern Ireland. Sims convinced Admiral Bayly that the way to beat the U-boat menace was the convoy system. At that time, merchant ships crossed the ocean singly or in small groups. Dispersed, they were difficult to guard and easy prey for the submarines. But packed together

Revolutionaries known as Bolsheviks incited the Russian people to rebel against the Government in 1917. The painting at left depicts a Bolshevik attack on the Winter Palace.

in a convoy, they could be given a heavy, concentrated guard of circling destroyers. This was what was done. Similar convoy operations were begun at Brest on the French coast and Gibraltar at the mouth of the Mediterranean.

Shipping losses were quickly cut in two, and by midsummer of 1917 America's military leaders felt confident that they could begin shipping men and arms to the battle without fear of torpedoes. But by that time also, Russia was on the way out of the war.

The year 1916 ended ominously for the Czar. On the night of December 29, a pair of Russian nobles murdered Rasputin (see page 100).

He was called the Mad Monk, this foul Siberian peasant, although he had never taken holy orders. His real name was Grigori Novikh, but he preferred the nickname Rasputin, which means "Dirty Dog." It was fitting. He began his career as a horse thief, town drunk, and chaser of women. Then he posed as a religious healer. He let his hair grow long and refused to wash in the name of "holiness." But Rasputin did have great hypnotic powers. This evil, reeking charmer was able to cast his spell upon the Czarina herself. He pretended to be able to heal the Czarina's ailing little son. Eventually, Rasputin was able to influence the highest councils of state. In Russia the road to wealth or power was paved with bribes to Rasputin. He was the chief corrupter of the corrupt Romanov dynasty.

Two avengers of Russian honor—Prince Yusupov and Grand Duke Dimitri Pavlovich—conspired to

kill Rasputin. They invited him to dinner. They plied him with vodka laced with cyanide. He kept on drinking. They emptied a pistol into him. Rasputin still lived. In desperation, they lugged him out onto the frozen Neva River and dropped him through a hole in the ice. That was the end of Rasputin, and it is sometimes referred to as the first act in the Russian Revolution.

Rasputin's executioners boasted openly of their deed. They had defied the Czar and the vengeful Czarina. From that time onward, imperial Russia sank into chaos.

Street rioting broke out in the capital at Petrograd (now Leningrad) in late February, 1917. On March 8, hungry rioters sacked the city's bakery shops. Three days later, troops were called out to break the riots, but the soldiers shot their officers and joined the mob. Next day all of the 190,000 soldiers stationed in Petrograd joined the mutiny. The revolution was in full swing. The Winter Palace was invaded, public buildings were burned, and the fortress of St. Peter and St. Paul was thrown open and prisoners were freed.

The revolt spread from city to city and it became apparent that the guiding force was the Council of Workmen's and Soldiers' Delegates (the Soviet). On March 14, a distraught Czar Nicholas II called in one of his top generals and asked: "What shall I do?"

The answer came back not from the military but from the Duma: "You must abdicate!"

Czar Nicholas and Czarina Alexandra were photographed surrounded by their handsome family (left) before the revolution. After his abdication, the forlorn ex-ruler (right) was held in detention on the grounds of an estate known as Tsarkoe Selo. Behind him, soldiers stand guard.

The next day two Duma members—Basil Shulgin and War Minister Alexander Guchkov—came to visit the Czar aboard the royal train.

"You must abdicate in favor of your son," Guchkov told the Czar.

"I can't be separated from my boy," the Czar answered. "I will leave the throne to my brother [the Grand Duke Michael]. Give me a piece of paper."

His aides brought him paper, and he wrote out his abdication.

The Czar's piece of paper, however, meant nothing to the Petrograd Soviet. Instead of Grand Duke Michael, a Provisional Government began to rule Russia. Its prime minister was Prince Georgi Lvov, and the Socialist Alexander Kerensky was one of its members. But true power resided in the Soviet. This was made plain by Guchkov, who wrote to the commander of the Russian Army: "The Provisional Government's orders are executed only so far as this is permitted by the Soviet, which holds in its hands the important elements, the troops, the railroads, the postal and telegraph services."

Within that Petrograd Soviet was a small minority of members known as the Bolsheviks, who stood for the violent overthrow of the capitalist system. During that momentous March, their leader was far away in exile.

He called himself Lenin, but his real name was Vladimir Ilyich Ulyanov. He was the arch-

CONTINUED ON PAGE 96

Revolutionary soldiers with bayonets board a truck in the snowy streets of Petrograd (Leningrad) during the rioting of March, 1917. The Government was paralyzed as the

*rioting swiftly spread to other Russian cities. The discontent of the people forced the
abdication of weak-willed Nicholas, thus ending the three-century rule of the Romanovs.*

revolutionary, a man of many and profound hatreds. Lenin hated imperialist Russia because his brother, another revolutionary, had been executed at the Czar's command. He hated capitalist society because he believed in the Communist creed of the German philosopher Karl Marx. According to Marxism, the proletariat—the laboring or wage-earning class—was to destroy the property-owning classes, whom the Communists call the bourgeoisie.

When Lenin heard of the fall of the Czar, he recognized that this was his chance to put his revolutionary plan into effect. Immediately he got off a cable to his Bolshevik followers in the Petrograd Soviet: "Our tactics—no support, complete contempt. Armed proletariat, only guarantee." In other words, Lenin was already plotting the overthrow of the Provisional Government. Next, he got in touch with German officials to request transportation back to Russia! It was a clever and audacious move, and no less a personage than Erich Ludendorff also thought that it was a good idea. A peerless rabble-rouser such as Lenin ought to speed Russia's exit from the war.

The request was granted. A train with special privileges was furnished Lenin and his handful of followers. No German officials would board it as it passed through Germany or German-held territory, and no one would be permitted to get off. On April 9, like a great sealed black box loaded with the deadly political virus of Communism, the train left Zurich for Petrograd.

There, Lenin made it clear that he wanted complete power. He would associate himself with the Provisional Government only in order to bring it down. To Lenin, as to all of his heirs, the word "negotiate" was to mean not give-and-take but simply take. A movement or organization was to be joined solely to wreck or control it. And everything that Lenin did suited the designs of General Ludendorff.

"What do you get out of war?" the fiery revolutionary would shout nightly at throngs of Russians. "Only wounds, starvation, and death!"

Then, as if to confirm his message of pacifism, Russian soldiers (who had enjoyed some success in one last offensive during the summer of 1917) flatly refused to obey their officers. They threw down their

Russian troops, after hearing the news of a German cavalry breakthrough, throw down their arms and flee from the battlefield (above). A soldier still loyal to the army (right) attempts to force his comrades to return to duty. Similar scenes occurred throughout every division of the Russian Army. Although the leaders of the Provisional Government believed that a great offensive against the Germans would be Russia's salvation, the war-weary soldiers quit. They were imbued with the spirit of revolutionary leaders who wanted peace.

Alexander Kerensky (photographed above reading a map) was the strong man of the Provisional Government, which replaced the Czar. Kerensky planned the great offensive in Galicia that bore his name. It was the last battle fought by Russia in the war.

weapons and went home. Gradually, as Lenin's influence in the Petrograd Soviet grew, the strength of the Provisional Government waned. Russian defeats on the battlefield helped to discredit the new popular idol, Alexander Kerensky.

Soon, Lenin had control of the Soviet, and his lieutenant, Leon Trotsky, controlled the one in Moscow. Lenin thereupon summoned an All-Russian Congress of Soviets to meet in Petrograd the first week in November. Before it did, the army regiments stationed in Petrograd adopted this resolu-

Nikolai Lenin (right) and Leon Trotsky (below in the fur hat) gave leadership to Russian masses in revolt. Lenin wears a workman's cap, showing his sympathy with the proletariat.

tion: "We no longer recognize the Provisional Government. The Petrograd Soviet is our Government."

It was the trumpet blast of Communism on the march. Lenin heard it and ordered full-scale revolt. In a two-day takeover that was almost devoid of either drama or combat, Kerensky was forced to leave Russia, and the Communists with Lenin at their head seized power.

Appearing before the Soviet Congress now assembled, Nikolai Lenin read a decree calling for a "just and democratic peace."

"The war is ended!" the delirious delegates chanted. "The war is ended!"

It was only then that France and England and the United States began to realize that they were in danger of losing their Eastern ally. But by then it was too late to remedy the situation.

"We don't want a separate peace," Leon Trotsky told the Allied ambassadors, "but peace we must have, and if we can't seek it together, the blame is on you."

Supremely confident, the Communists sent their delegates to confer with the Germans at Brest Litovsk. A few days there and the Communist self-assurance was rudely jolted. Germany would grant peace, but only in exchange for the partition of Poland and Russia's Baltic provinces. Stunned,

Before the end came for the Russian Army, some women were volunteering for military duty. In the photograph at right, a fur-hatted general inspects a battalion consisting mainly of war widows. Other Russian women took the places of their husbands on the farms and in the factories. The defeats of 1916 and the revolutionary events of 1917 were hard on women of all classes, but to the ladies of the decadent Romanov court, they were disastrous. The photograph above, showing a group of gentlewomen fawning on the influential monk Rasputin before his assassination, is thus a memorial to a government that was too degenerate to exist in the modern world.

the Communist delegates returned to Petrograd.

In mid-January of 1918 they were back with the confident Leon Trotsky at their head. All of Trotsky's persuasiveness could not budge the Germans, however. They wanted eighteen Russian provinces for the Kaiser. In that case, Trotsky said, Russia would simply leave the war without making peace with Germany. He had the naïve dream that Germany would not make war on a country that had laid down her arms. He was mistaken. Ludendorff ordered General Max von Hoffmann to resume the war in the East.

Again the field-gray columns moved forward in Russia, but this time against no opposition. "It's the most comical war I've ever known," General Hoffmann wrote. "We put a handful of men on a train with a machine gun, run them into a town, and they capture it."

Soon the entire Ukraine—the breadbasket of Russia—was in German hands. Frantic, Lenin and Trotsky notified Hoffmann that they would sign on Germany's terms. Hoffmann ignored it, and kept his troops rolling. By February 21, German soldiers had landed in Finland and defeated the Red Guards in Helsinki. Across the Gulf of Finland were the onion-shaped spires of Petrograd. Lenin and Trotsky capitulated. At the end of February a cowed Communist delegation was back in Brest Litovsk.

On March 3, 1918, Russia made peace with Germany. Under the terms demanded by the insatiable Ludendorff, Russia yielded 34 per cent of her population, 32 per cent of her farmland, 50 per cent of her industrial holdings, and 90 per cent of her coal mines. Trotsky declared: "This is a peace that Russia, grinding her teeth, is forced to accept."

If Trotsky meant that the Russians would accept German terms while waiting for their vengeance, he was right. The new Communist rulers were buying time with space, time in which to consolidate themselves so that they might eventually try to recover the lost land. Trotsky also forged the Red Army, which in 1918 beat back a feeble postwar attempt of the Allies to purge the world of Communism.

So ended the second of two great events that were to change not only the course of the war but also the course of world history. In March and April, 1917, the Germans had sunk American ships and the United States had embarked on her career as a world power. In the same period, Czarism ended and Nikolai Lenin left Zurich in his sealed train.

The world would never be the same again.

Shortly before the outbreak of war, a division of Russia's great army proudly passes in review before visiting French dignitaries on a field near St. Petersburg (below). Well-trained and properly equipped, the infantry struts across the parade ground followed by the cavalry. Several years later little was left of these huge forces. Their supplies depleted, their spirit broken, they were a defeated army. A German war artist's sketch of downcast Russian prisoners (far right) captures the abject mood of the once-mighty army.

L'ILLUSTRATION

As four French soldiers (top) approach German trenches in Champagne, one man (right background) is shot down. The unsuccessful French offensives of 1917 increased dissatisfaction among the troops. Badly mauled armies were repeatedly sent back into battle.

MUTINY

10

It was a fateful day for England and for France when, in December, 1916, General Robert Nivelle took command of the French armies.

General Nivelle's confidence in his own ability was rivaled only by his charming way with politicians. Both Premier Aristide Briand of France and Prime Minister David Lloyd George of Britain believed that Nivelle was the answer to their prayers. They did not understand that the new chief's victories at Verdun had been small-scale successes against limited objectives. Nor were they aware that Nivelle had little experience in high command. Therefore, when "the Nivelle Offensive" was proposed, they were solidly behind it.

The Nivelle system, of which the General was so proud, was merely to assemble his troops in secret and attack without a prolonged bombardment that would warn the enemy of a big push. In this way, Nivelle hoped, great masses of infantry attacking on a wide front would achieve surprise.

Actually, aside from the element of surprise, his plan was hardly different from previous ones. Nivelle was after the Germans who were positioned within a bulge between Arras in the north and Soissons in the south. Sir Douglas Haig with his British, plus some French divisions, would attack in the north, while three French armies would strike from the south. The idea was to meet behind the Germans, cut them off, and thus tear a huge hole in the German line (see map on page 63).

"We will win it all," General Nivelle said confidently, "within twenty-four to forty-eight hours."

Nivelle's confidence led him to circulate his plan widely. The tight security on which his plan depended was totally lacking. Moreover, it was impossible to make huge concentrations of troops secretly, and the Germans quickly learned of the Big Push scheduled for the spring of 1917.

To forestall it, they simply pulled back. They evacuated their salient within the Allied line. Before they left, they made a desert of the land they had held. Thousands of homes were pulled down, orchards leveled, forests burned, bridges blown, railroads undermined, roads wiped out, and reservoirs and wells poisoned.

Thus, it was no longer possible for Nivelle to envelop the enemy. The Germans had shortened their front by twenty-seven miles, in effect adding eight divisions to their strength. Moreover, they had taken up new positions to the rear in what was called the Hindenburg Line. Ludendorff had out-

Jaunty General Nivelle (above) insisted on pursuing his plan for a spring offensive in 1917 even after the German withdrawal to the Hindenburg Line made such an attack unwise.

Nivelle's grand-scale attack, begun on April 16, quickly bogged down, inflicting on the troops the usual grim number of casualties. At right, a group of medical corpsmen evacuate the British wounded from behind the battle line. After two futile weeks, French soldiers stopped fighting and began to mutiny. At left, men are shown deserting the front lines.

maneuvered Nivelle. But Nivelle was undaunted, even on receiving reports of German reinforcement.

"The greater their numbers the greater my victory," he argued.

Two ranking generals did not agree. General Alfred Micheler, who commanded the three French armies in the south, felt that the German pull-back had knocked the plan into a cocked hat. General Pétain also objected. At a showdown conference of political and military chiefs, Pétain said: "We have not the means to carry it out. Even if we were to succeed, we could not exploit it. Have we five hundred thousand fresh troops for the advance? No. Then it is impossible."

General Nivelle jumped to his feet and shouted: "Since I do not have the confidence either of the Government or of my subordinates, the only course open is to resign." At once the politicians gathered around to smooth his ruffled feathers. No one dared to call his bluff, and preparations for the ill-fated Nivelle Offensive went forward.

In the north, Haig's British-French force rammed ahead in an effort to draw German divisions up to that sector. The result was that Sir Douglas lost another 177,000 men. A week later, the French armies in the south went plunging ahead—straight into similar disaster: 187,000 men lost. General Nivelle, who had promised to call off his push if it did not immediately succeed, kept the battle raging for ten days. When he had to accept defeat, he attempted

to shift the blame onto General Micheler's shoulders. Micheler lashed back:

"What, you try to make me responsible for the mistake, when I never ceased to warn you? Do you know what such an action is called? It is called cowardice!"

That was the end of General Nivelle, and it was also nearly the end of the French Army.

Mutiny flared. It began on April 29 in one regiment and swept like a plague through the rest of the army. Nivelle's blood bath had been the last straw. Rioting troops threw down their weapons and set up noncommissioned officers' committees to replace their officers. In some areas they simply deserted, ran off to the rear, or refused to go forward when ordered. Others got so drunk they could not move in any direction. At no time, however, did the enraged *poilus* ever shoot their officers.

"We will not harm you," one *poilu* with thirty-two months of battle duty to his credit told a lieutenant. "You have been abused as much as we have. But we will not obey you. The war must end."

Into this dreadful and delicate situation strode General Pétain, the savior of Verdun and the man who had openly opposed Nivelle. Even Pétain's enormous popularity was put to the test, however. He had to suppress a mutiny, and that meant being harsh. But he could not long continue the executions that had been begun by drumhead courts shooting mutineers out of hand, for he also had to nurse a demoralized army back to health—and that meant being kind. In the end, Pétain did succeed in striking a balance between these two extremes. Of the thousands of men brought to trial under his direction, only twenty-three are known to have been executed. On the other hand, Pétain's leniency put about a third of the French Army on furlough, the living conditions were greatly improved, and the *poilu* was given to understand that soldiers' lives were no longer to be wasted so wantonly.

1

2

4

5

Sir William Orpen, an official war artist, visited British headquarters in France in the spring of 1917. The object of the visit was to paint a portrait of Sir Douglas Haig. On Haig's advice Orpen went to the front to sketch survivors of the Battle of Arras. Four of his black and white studies of battle-fatigued soldiers are reproduced here: (2) a weary soldier rests his head in his hands; (4) a new recruit in kilts already dazed with shock; (6) a private getting some rest along the roadside; (8) a man staring into space, bewildered by the horror he has seen.

8

3

French artist Jean Lefort painted the front line soldier with accuracy and compassion. His water color miniatures were made in a pocket-size sketchbook that he kept from 1915 to 1918. Among his up-front impressions are (1) an artillery column moving out of Noyon in March, 1917; (3) a pipe-smoking potato-peeler sharing mess duty with a companion; (5) a pack-laden trio in the rain; (7) two infantrymen clasping hands as they pass each other; (9) a wounded man being brought down into the trench.

6

7

9

The brawny machine gunner painted by official War Department artist Harvey Dunn exudes the self-assurance that doughboys brought with them to France. The arrival of American troops revived the Allies' sagging spirits.

WE'RE COMING OVER 11

The French had hoped to hush up news of the mutiny. Although it was in full swing during that very summer of 1917 when General Pershing arrived in France, the A.E.F. commander knew nothing of it. However, the British suspected that something was wrong.

During a meeting between Pétain and Lloyd George, the General said: "I suppose you think I can't fight." The Prime Minister replied: "No, General, but for some reason or other, you won't fight."

Eventually, the British came to know of the French troops' rebellion, and Sir Douglas Haig used the fact of an ailing ally as an excuse to launch another big push. Haig argued that the B.E.F. had better strike before the Germans could crash through the French position. He chose again the Ypres sector, and began the preliminaries to the third battle of that name—the one that is also called (by the British) the Battle of Passchendaele.

The Messines Ridge was held by the Germans alongside the British bulge at Ypres (see map on page 112). If the B.E.F. could seize this key feature, they could pivot on it, swinging north to liberate the whole Belgian coast. The attack was to be launched with a monster explosion that had been in preparation for two years.

During that time, the British Second Army under General Sir Herbert Plumer had been stealthily undermining the German position. Molelike sappers had dug five miles of galleries under the unsuspecting Germans' very feet. They had stuffed these tunnels with one million pounds of explosives. On the night of June 6, Sir Herbert called a press conference and said: "Gentlemen, I don't know whether we will make history tomorrow, but we will certainly change geography."

At 3:10 the next morning the lever was pressed. Nineteen huge mines went off as one, and far away Lloyd George in his study at 10 Downing Street heard the rumble and felt the shock. Craters a hundred yards wide and a hundred feet deep had been blasted in the earth. Some twenty thousand German soldiers had been killed or wounded, and those who survived were found wandering about gibbering in terror.

Quickly the Tommies in their flat-brimmed helmets pressed forward. By dusk they had reached their first day's objectives and taken thousands of prisoners. As it had been ever since the Battle of the Marne, however, the Germans recovered and began counterattacking. British casualties rose. Undaunted, General Haig launched his main drive for the Belgian coast on July 31. Another great wasting effort was under way and it would rage on fruitlessly until the third week in November, when adverse weather brought the fighting to an end.

Passchendaele cost Britain an additional 245,000 men. Instead of sweeping to the Belgian coast, Sir Douglas Haig acquired about nine thousand yards of shell-pocked, bloody mire. Obviously, new techniques—and more and more men—would be needed if victory was ever to be won.

"We're coming over, We're coming over—
And we won't be back till it's over, over there."

So sang the Yanks, a few hundred thousand strong now, trudging over the dusty roads of France, bellowing out war ballads and ditties as they marched. They were a high-hearted, high-spirited army, these doughboys of the A.E.F. When they were not singing, they were talking. One of their

111

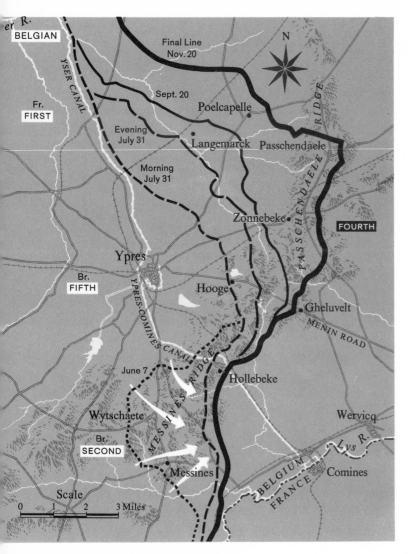

favorite sayings was, "Start arguin', boys!" They did not complain much. Their Uncle Sam did not pay them generously, and he gave them no more than clothes, bedding, a toothbrush, and a safety razor. Yet they served him with a simple faith in the nobility of their cause. They did not think they were supposed to "get something" out of their service. Although they were individualists and were not too fond of spit-and-polish, they accepted discipline and obeyed orders.

Of course they beefed. All good soldiers do. They wished the man who designed their uniform would die a painful death. It was trim and natty looking, well enough, but its choker collar shut off air, its tight tunic was hot and stiff, and the tape puttees wound around their legs cut off circulation. They also said uncomplimentary things about the food served them. Still, they kept their sense of humor, inventing such things as the Order of the Cootie.

Sir Douglas Haig set in motion a plan to reduce the Ypres salient on July 31, 1917. The Third Battle of Ypres, or Passchendaele, is shown on the map at left: black lines mark the successive stages of the four-month struggle. As in prior battles, little ground was gained but many lives were lost. Below left, British stretcher bearers, up to their knees in mud, carry an Ypres casualty. Advancing Canadians, bayonets ready, go over the top, below right.

Any man who had been to the front and picked up his share of body lice or "cooties" was eligible to join this select group.

When the doughboys fought they whooped it up like a crowd of boys playing football, and the first ones to do so were the men of the battalion that had marched in Paris.

In late October, 1917, the 1st Infantry Division went into line on one of the quiet sectors near the Swiss border. There had been little fighting in this region since the war began. Every evening there was a mutual exchange of shells, all carefully aimed at open fields. A *poilu* might wash his underwear on a sunny day and hang it out in full view of the German soldiers across the way, confident that no sniper's bullet would cut him down. Did not the *Boche* do the same?

But then *les Américains* had come bursting into this quiet truce with all the unsettling impact of a shell from Big Bertha. "Every man in the 1st Division wanted to go on a patrol, and then a raid," wrote Laurence Stallings, the chronicler of the doughboy in France. "Each wanted to kill a German, to capture one, to be the first."

So the French were glad to withdraw when the tall soldiers of the 1st Division came marching in. A German assault company came up to investigate the goings on. These were elite troops, specialists in hit-and-run raids. They were going to test those brash Yanks who did not aim their artillery at open fields but at crowded trenches. On the night of November 2, fresh battalions of the 1st Division came into line. The dugouts were already muddy with autumn rains. The new arrivals, weighted down by their long rain-soaked overcoats, slipped and sloshed in their unfamiliar surroundings. By midnight they had settled down. By then, the German assault company had also established itself opposite the battalion that had marched to Lafayette's grave in Paris.

At three in the morning the German artillery opened up. Tons of metal fell about the Yank battalion. Soon the barrage shifted, seeking and finding its target: F Company, 2nd Battalion, 16th Infantry. It cut the company off from its fellow units in a fearful box barrage. Then the box barrage deliberately isolated a platoon chosen for the assault company's attack. Now the night was shrieking and crashing with the explosion of eight-inch mortar shells. Nothing now could come to the aid of this isolated platoon of fifty-eight men.

Two hundred yards opposite them were the as-

saulters. Knives sharpened, Lugers loaded, grenades primed, they started forward. Bangalore torpedoes forced a way open through the American barbed wire, and they kept coming. Now the side of the box barrage that was nearest to the Germans vanished. The other three sides, to the flanks and rear of the doughboys, continued to erupt.

Out of the dark came the assaulters, yelling wildly. They leaped into the American trenches. They expected the surprised defenders to turn and flee. But no Americans turned tail. They stood and fought. Three minutes after the attack had started, the assaulters withdrew.

Taking their own dead and wounded, they dragged off eleven stunned Americans. Then the front of the box barrage closed in again. Pursuit was impossible. Three minutes later the Germans and their prisoners were safely within their own lines, and the box barrage lifted.

In the strange and eerie silence that comes upon the end of combat, the Americans took stock of themselves. Forty-four men were still on their feet. Eleven men—the prisoners—were missing. Three doughboys lay dead on the floor of the trench. They were Corporal James B. Gresham, Private Thomas F. Enright, and Private Merle D. Hay. They were the first Americans to die in World War I.

They and their brave companions had given their reply to the question that the Germans had been asking themselves: Would the Americans fight?

They would.

Other American outfits had their first taste of battle in that fall of 1917, and more new American divisions arrived in France. The spirits of the Allies lifted. But then came news of Italian disaster. Fresh German divisions had been fed into the Austrian Army. Between October 24 and November 12, this spearhead drove into Italy itself.

At the Battle of Caporetto the Austro-Germans broke the Italian Army into pieces. Some 305,000 Italians were lost, of whom 275,000 surrendered. The fleeing Italian Army dissolved into a rabble of panicky soldiers sweeping a terrified citizenry before them (see overleaf).

British and French divisions had to be rushed to Italy to keep that nation in the war. King Victor Emmanuel II tried to rally his people. "Citizens and soldiers, be a single army," he cried. "All cowardice is treachery, all discord is treachery." Helped by a

CONTINUED ON PAGE 118

114

American troops arriving in Europe were ill-prepared for the battle techniques required along an established front. Pershing ordered them to be put through rigorous training in France in both trench and open warfare. On the opposite page, men of the 82nd Division advance across a field under simulated gunfire. Above, a smaller group struggles through rough terrain learning the fine points of a raid.

A spearhead of Austrian and German troops drove into Italy in the fall of 1917 and smashed the Italian Army at Caporetto. Remnants of the defeated forces (left) began a retreat that lasted three weeks and covered 60 miles. A description of the vanquished army was written by Ernest Hemingway, a volunteer ambulance driver with the Italian Army, in A Farewell to Arms. "The retreat was orderly, wet, and sullen. In the night, going slowly along the crowded roads we passed troops marching under the rain, guns, horses pulling wagons . . . all moving away from the front."

117

Milan editor named Benito Mussolini, the King gradually restored order. Poor weather and the lack of bridging materials also slowed the Austro-Germans. When it became apparent that the conquest could not be completed before winter, Ludendorff recalled his divisions to the western front.

Italy's near collapse, however, coincided with the Communist takeover in Russia. With one ally, Italy, faltering, and another, Russia, about to decamp, the Allies decided to call a council of war. It assembled at Rapallo in Italy. Lloyd George was there for England, Premier Paul Painlevé for France, Prime Minister Vittorio E. Orlando for Italy, and Colonel Edward M. House represented President Wilson. They formed the Supreme War Council to direct the war. It would correct the lack of unity that had always plagued the Allies. From this meeting would come the unified command that was so badly needed.

After it adjourned, Georges Clemenceau emerged as the new Premier of France. He was the one leader who could revive his weary country, and he already had his eye on the one man capable of holding the over-all military command: Ferdinand Foch.

A fresh will to victory was taking hold of the Allies.

While the Allied command was changing in Italy, the very nature of warfare itself was changing in France.

At the little Battle of Cambrai fought in late November, 1917, the English tentatively introduced the use of massed tanks moving ahead of infantry. Brigadier General Sir Hugh Elles had gathered 324 tanks in his Tank Corps. Two thirds of these were to spearhead a force of twelve infantry divisions. The other tanks were put in reserve.

In 1917 the British first used large forces of tanks in the inconclusive Battle of Cambrai. There it was learned that tanks alone were not enough—tanks and infantry had to be used together. In the photograph at left, American troops advance backed by tanks in a training maneuver. A great success was scored by the doughboys and tanks at Cantigny in 1918. At right, a contemporary cartoon hails the victory.

The target was southwest of Cambrai (see map on page 168). Here the countryside is a chalky plain laced with small streams and dikes. Such firm ground is made for the movement of tanks. General Sir Julian Byng, who commanded the attack, hoped to surprise the Germans. There would be no preliminary bombardment. The tanks would emerge out of the cover of a smoke screen. To get across deep trenches dug by the Germans as an antitank obstacle, each British tank carried bundles of sticks to be dropped in the ditches as makeshift bridges.

All this was done, and Cambrai was a great success. There was no attempt to make a deeper penetration. Still, more ground was won at Cambrai in one day than was won during the four bloody months of Third Ypres; there were only four thousand British casualties. Eventually, the Germans began to counterattack the shoulders of the British

salient, regaining most of the ground that they had lost and forcing the Tommies to withdraw.

But the British soldier had shown the world how to break the stalemate on the western front. The world, however, or at least the High Command, was blind. No military chief on either side appreciated the significance of what had happened at Cambrai. Only General Elles and his brilliant second, Colonel J. F. C. Fuller, understood that the problem that had faced warfare since the invention of firearms had been solved by the tank.

This was simply how to advance the guns under enemy rifle or machine gun fire. Heretofore, artillery always had to be kept back of the line. Any soldiers attempting to haul artillery into the battle would be quickly picked off. However, point-blank artillery fire is the most effective of all weapons. It not only slaughters, it terrifies. The idea of a continuous

119

advance of big guns spewing death is simply too much for any soldier to bear.

Tanks are nothing less than artillery. But they are self-propelled and they are armored. Therefore, they can advance against enemy rifle or machine gun fire. Moreover, the approach of tanks is a continuous advance. As Colonel Fuller was to write later, the advance of tanks would be not just overwhelmingly destructive but overwhelmingly demoralizing. And because battles are won and lost not by killing soldiers but by making soldiers throw down their arms and run, the tank was the answer to modern warfare.

All this General Elles and Colonel Fuller knew, but they were not in a position to give decisive orders. It remained for another world war and another German Army to take up the lessons laid down by Fuller. Position warfare was to continue. Worse, the war itself was to continue, despite the fact that the end to the stalemate seemed to be nowhere in sight.

At the end of 1917 peace feelers were sent out from Vienna. The Austrians asked General Ludendorff if Germany would be willing to return the provinces of Alsace and Lorraine to France. Ludendorff's reply was a resounding "Never!"

Thus ended the critical year 1917. America had entered the war and Russia was leaving it. Communism had emerged while Fascism was still only a superpatriotic emotion locked in the breast of Benito Mussolini. Submarine warfare, the German weapon of victory, had failed to starve the Allies, while the British blockade was visiting starvation upon the German people. Tank warfare, the Allies' weapon of victory, lay idle in their hands. Someone had cried, "Peace!" and the cruel Ludendorff had growled in reply, "War!"

Hereafter, war was to mean total war.

120

The first tanks of World War I were clumsy vehicles, but their caterpillar treads allowed them to ride over the trenches and their armor protected them from machine gun fire, an advantage troops did not have. Later models developed by the Allies and used at Amiens (above) in 1918 had greater speed and thicker armor than their ancestors. At left, a water color depicts another model, with shorter treads, battered out of commission on the western front.

The airplane gave another new, exciting but dreadful, dimension to warfare. Above, British Bristol F-2B fighters fly over Serny Airfield en route to the German lines.

WAR IN THE AIR 12

Again it was the Kaiser, the man who had launched sink-on-sight submarine warfare, who added another brutal innovation to the horrors of World War I: the systematic bombing of civilian centers. German aircraft made small raids on English cities throughout 1914, and at the start of 1915 big naval Zeppelins began bombing London.

The Zeppelins were airships named after the German count who was a pioneer in lighter-than-air aviation. They were dirigibles—that is, huge sausage-shaped structures filled with gas to make them ride as buoyantly in the sky as ships upon the sea. They were driven by propellers controlled from a cabin slung beneath their bellies. They were terrifying and, at first, woefully effective in carrying out their missions of death and destruction.

Gradually, however, the British beat back the Zeppelin menace. Antiaircraft guns and high-powered searchlights were developed. Blackouts were introduced. And, even more importantly, fighter planes were sent aloft equipped with guns that could rip through the thin skins of the expensive and cumbrous monsters.

But it was only recently that the airplane had come to be considered important as a weapon. Although the United States had what was in effect the world's first air force, it consisted, until 1911, of only one plane and one pilot. It was a very small part of the Army Signal Corps and it was allowed $150 a year for fuel and repairs!

By the onset of World War I, most generals regarded their airplanes as the "eyes" of the army. They used them for observation. Pilots flew over enemy territory to spy on enemy movements, or else they directed artillery fire. The airplane did not seem to be a weapon at all, but rather a useful machine like a truck.

Yet, before the end of 1914, it was clear to both sides that something had to be done to prevent air attacks and to stop aerial spying. Antiaircraft guns were last-ditch defenses, and ground fire rarely, if ever, damaged an observation plane. So both alliances sought to develop an airplane to fight other airplanes—with greater speed, more firepower, and increased maneuverability.

Although the Germans, French, and English were all soon able to design and produce speedy, maneuverable aircraft, it was some time before the firepower problem could be solved. In the beginning, men in airplanes shot at each other with rifles. Then machine guns were mounted on the topmost wing of biplanes. In 1915, the Dutch designing genius Anthony Fokker came up with a swift monoplane with machine guns synchronized to fire through its propeller. His little Fokkers ruled the skies for Germany. But then one of them was shot down in Allied territory and the secret was out.

New Allied planes that also were able to deliver straight-ahead fire began rolling off the assembly line. French Nieuports and Spads, British Sopwith Camels and de Haviland II's, they were all able to engage the Fokker on even terms.

Growling dogfights became common above the western front, and a new type of warrior hero was

A painting by N. G. Arnold recaptures a vivid moment in the air war of 1917: a squadron of German planes is greeted by British antiaircraft fire over the domes of London.

born. He was the fighter pilot, glamorous in his leather helmet and goggles, his silk scarf streaming in the wind. There was a new kind of military shop-talk: doing "loops" or making "Immelmanns" (the turn invented by the German ace Max Immelmann). Even an "ace"—a man who had five victories to his credit—was something new.

Britain, of course, emerged from the war as the strongest air power. She had begun with 63 airplanes to 200 for the Germans, and with only 1,889 officers and men. By the war's end, Britain had 22,000 aircraft and an independent Royal Air Force of 291,175 officers and men.

Americans were in on aerial warfare early, even though their nation remained neutral for nearly three years. By special arrangement so that they would not lose their citizenship, they were permitted to join the French Flying Corps. Their unit was the

Lafayette Escadrille, and it became famous. Men such as Kiffin Yates Rockwell, Norman Prince, Victor Chapman, William Thaw, Bert Hall, and Raoul Lufbery wrote history in the skies. In all, the fliers of the Lafayette Escadrille claimed 199 German aircraft destroyed against 51 of their own pilots killed.

After America entered the war, the Lafayette Escadrille was disbanded, and its pilots joined the new American units being formed. One of these outfits was the famous 94th "Hat in the Ring" Pursuit Squadron, stationed near Toul in France. On April 14, 1918, the Hat in the Ring pilots made the first American combat patrol.

At dawn of that date Captain Peterson led Lieutenants Reed Chambers and Eddie Rickenbacker aloft over Saint-Mihiel. Below on stand-by duty were Lieutenants Alan Winslow and Douglas Campbell. A thick fog closed in. Chambers became tem-

CONTINUED ON PAGE 128

124

PUBLIC WARNING

The public are advised to familiarise themselves with the appearance of British and German Airships and Aeroplanes, so that they may not be alarmed by British aircraft, and may take shelter if German aircraft appear. **Should hostile aircraft be seen,** take shelter **immediately** in the nearest available house, preferably in the basement, and remain there until the aircraft have left the vicinity: do not stand about in crowds **and do not touch unexploded bombs.**

In the event of **HOSTILE** aircraft being seen in country districts, the nearest Naval, Military or Police Authorities should, if possible, be advised immediately by Telephone of the TIME OF APPEARANCE, the DIRECTION OF FLIGHT, **and whether the aircraft is an Airship or an Aeroplane.**

GERMAN

AIRSHIPS

BRITISH

AIRSHIPS

Note specially the shape of the Airships and the position of the passenger cars

ZEPPELIN

SCHÜTTE - LANZ

PARSEVAL

H.M.A. ASTRA TORRES

H.M.A. BETA

H.M.A. ETA

H.M.A. PARSEVAL

Note specially the sloped-back wings of the German Aeroplanes

AEROPLANES

AEROPLANES

STAHLTAUBE MONOPLANE

RUMPLER TAUBE MONOPLANE

AVIATIK BIPLANE

ALBATROSS BIPLANE

D.F.W. BIPLANE

BRISTOL BIPLANE

BRISTOL BIPLANE

AVRO BIPLANE

AVRO BIPLANE

SHORT BIPLANE

B.E. BIPLANE

SOPWITH TRACTOR BIPLANE

H. FARMAN BIPLANE

SOPWITH TRACTOR BIPLANE

LONDON:
PRINTED UNDER THE AUTHORITY OF HIS MAJESTY'S STATIONERY OFFICE.
By SIR JOSEPH CAUSTON & SONS, LIMITED, 9, Eastcheap, E.C.

To be purchased, either directly or through any Bookseller, from WYMAN & SONS, LIMITED, 29, Breams Buildings, Fetter Lane, E.C., and 54, St. Mary Street, Cardiff; or H.M. STATIONERY OFFICE (Scottish Branch), 23, Forth Street, Edinburgh; or E. PONSONBY, LIMITED, 116, Grafton Street, Dublin; or from the Agencies in the British Colonies and Dependencies, the United States of America, the Continent of Europe and Abroad of T. FISHER UNWIN, London, W.C.
1915.
PRICE TWOPENCE

COPYRIGHT
Sir Joseph Causton
& Sons, Ltd.
London

This British identification poster helped civilians distinguish between friendly and enemy aircraft.

126

The fallen Zeppelin LZ-49 lies in a French field after having been shot down in October, 1917. By that time the Germans had begun to replace the huge dirigibles with winged

*bombers. Zeppelins had been used by the Germans mainly to carry large bomb loads;
they also carried strafing guns in the engine mounts that were slung beneath the hull.*

porarily lost, and Peterson and Rickenbacker were forced back to base to refuel.

Enemy motors were heard overhead. Instantly, the stand-by pilots—Winslow and Campbell—gunned their Spads down the runway and went roaring into the soup. Above the clouds they saw their prey: two German Fokkers. Guns flaming, they attacked. The Germans fought back.

Below, men at the American air base and the townspeople of Toul gazed upward in anxiety. Suddenly, a plane came plummeting out of the fog. It was a German! Another fell. It too was German. Both planes crashed, and Winslow and Campbell had earned the honor of scoring the first air victories for an American squadron.

Thereafter, the 94th was the scourge of the skies. Eddie Rickenbacker became the outstanding American ace with 26 victories.

Naturally, the Allied pilots who had been flying longer had much greater records. From England there was the great leader "Mick" Mannock, with 73 victories; James McCudden with 58; and nineteen-year-old Albert Ball with 43. Canada produced the superb Billy Bishop, who shot down 25 of his 72 kills within a twelve-day period. René Fonck of France was the Allied ace of aces, having 75 victories, while Georges Guynemer was a French legend. He had been refused by the army because of ill health, after which he took to the skies and shot down 53 Germans. Germany had Immelmann and Oswald Boelcke and Ernst Udet. There was also a heavy-set ace named Hermann Goering, who was to command Hitler's *Luftwaffe* in World War II. But the most famous name of all was that of the Red Knight, Baron Manfred von Richthofen. He flew an all-red plane at the head of his "circus," and he shot down 80 Allied aircraft before he was finally killed.

Eventually, the mission of the fighter plane was extended to include protection of bombers. The bomber itself was developed after the Germans realized that the huge Zeppelins of which they had been so proud were too vulnerable to ground fire and fighter attacks.

They switched to big bombers such as the Gotha and the Giant, and launched both daylight raids and moonlight strikes. Some of these planes were able to carry bombs weighing as much as 660

pounds. In all, the Germans killed thirteen hundred civilians and wounded another three thousand. They seriously disrupted the English war plant.

In retaliation, the Allies—chiefly Britain—launched air raids of their own. More and more German cities were attacked—Frankfort, Koblenz, Cologne, Mainz, Stuttgart, among others—and as the range of the British bombers grew longer, the bombs grew bigger. Before the war was over, the British had developed a bomb weighing 1,650

With aircraft, total warfare began; for the first time in history, attacks could be made far from the front lines. The Paris houses above were bombed out in March, 1918.

Eddie Rickenbacker, the highest ranking American ace, appears above at left beside his plane with its "Hat in the Ring" insignia. Other U.S. aces were Raoul Lufbery (at center) and Billy Mitchell (right). At top, Lufbery readies his plane for action.

129

pounds, and they were ready for raids on Berlin.

If the generals of World War I had been blind to the possibilities of the tank, they had by no means overlooked the airplane. Because of it, war had become total; whether in the trenches or in the streets, whether soldier or civilian, no one was safe.

130

An ace in a French biplane (foreground) watches as his burning German adversary starts to fall from the skies.

The conflagration that began in Europe finally broke out in every corner of the globe. Fighting men from Senegal, France, and Germany (top row, left to right), from Annam, India, and Great Britain (bottom row) represent some of the many faces of a world at war.

THE FLAMES
OF THE OUTER RIM

13

It *was* a world war. The flames fanned in Europe had spread to Asia and to Africa, ships had fought off both coasts of South America, from North America had come Canadian and Yankee armies, Japan moved into China and the Pacific—and the very water beneath the sea and the air above the earth were invaded by men with new and ingenious weapons in their hands.

Japan, of course, did not so much fight as go foraging. She declared war on Germany on August 23, 1914. Then she moved to obtain the territory of Kiaochow, which Germany had leased from China. Japanese battleships made a token bombardment of the area's port of Tsingtao, and the German governor pulled down his flag.

Next, Japan picked up Germany's island groups in the Pacific: the Marianas, Carolines, and Marshalls. Unfamiliar island names such as Kwajalein, Saipan, Guam, and Peleliu would one day become dreadfully familiar to another generation of Americans after the Japanese fortified them in preparation for another war. Japan also wanted the big island of Neu-Pommern near Australia. But the Australians got there first and renamed it New Britain.

Having driven the Kaiser from Asia and the Pacific, Japan sat down to digest her German meal.

Meanwhile, Germany was also being driven from her new possessions in Africa. Campaigns were launched against her in German Southwest Africa, German East Africa, and the German-held Cameroons. In the first, Germany had thought that the Dutch Boers of the Union of South Africa would not intervene in the war. It was believed that a nation only just conquered by Britain in the Boer War would not be eager to wield His Majesty's arms. But eager they were. Led by Generals Louis Botha

and Jan Christian Smuts, the South Africans—as they were now called—decisively defeated the German garrison.

In the east, the Germans struck first. They came out of German East Africa into British East Africa. Here, again, the South Africans came to the rescue. Joining a battalion of British Regulars, they helped win a victory in Uganda.

Meanwhile, a storybook battle was raging across the lakes and jungles of Central Africa. A pair of hostile gunboats could meet and decide the fate of a huge region. A body of mounted troops could do the same. For instance, German power around Lake Tanganyika was smashed by the unique feat of Commander G. Spicer Simson of the Royal Navy. He had two launches brought twenty-three hundred miles to the battle scene, sailing them up turbulent rivers and hauling them across malarial jungles. Another Englishman, Colonel P. V. Kelly, led his Third Hussars in a cavalry battle against the mounted tribesmen of pro-German Sultan Ali Dinar—killing the sultan and routing his army.

In the Cameroons, French and Belgian forces joined the British to sound the death knell of the Kaiser's ambitions in Africa. Except for isolated strong points that held out until near the war's end, the issue was resolved by 1916. The empire that vainglorious Kaiser Wilhelm had so hastily thrown together had fallen apart. In Asia still another rotten imperial structure—the ancient empire of the Ottomans—was also collapsing.

The Ottoman Empire from which modern Turkey is descended was once the terror of the world. It was ruled by the Turkish sultan, or sovereign. The Turks were a tribe from Central Asia

The GREATEST MOTHER in the WORLD

As battles raged at the front another kind of war was being fought behind the lines. The American Field Service, the Red Cross, the Norton-Harjes Ambulance Corps, and other agencies were working tirelessly to retrieve and save the injured. At left, Alonzo Earl Foringer's poster of a larger-than-life nurse cradling a wounded soldier summed up for many the wartime role of the Red Cross. Advance dressing stations like the one at right were busy round the clock.

that had been driven into Western Asia and Europe by the Mongols. Osman was their first sultan and his followers were called Osmanlis. Since "Ottoman" is the barbaric word for "Osmanli," the great imperial structure built by the Moslem Turks has been called the Ottoman Empire.

There was a time when this enormous Ottoman power threatened the very existence of Christendom and Western civilization: the Turks were at the gates of Vienna before they were repulsed. The Ottoman Empire once included much of the Middle East, Greece, the Balkans, Egypt, and most of the coast of North Africa. Its headquarters were in the old imperial Roman city of Constantinople, which since 1930 has been named Istanbul.

By the outbreak of World War I, the greater part of this empire had dwindled away. Turkey yearned to recover her lost dominions, and that is the reason Enver Pasha began his war against the Allies by attacking the Russian border to the north.

Before he did, he committed the last great outrage in the melancholy history of the Ottomans. He devastated the province of Armenia. The excuse was that Enver was planning to use Armenia as a base for the operation against Russia. He said he could not trust the Christian Armenians, who had been persecuted for centuries by their Moslem masters. Therefore, in 1915, he calmly ordered the slaughter of one million Armenians. Women were attacked, children sold into slavery, and old people driven

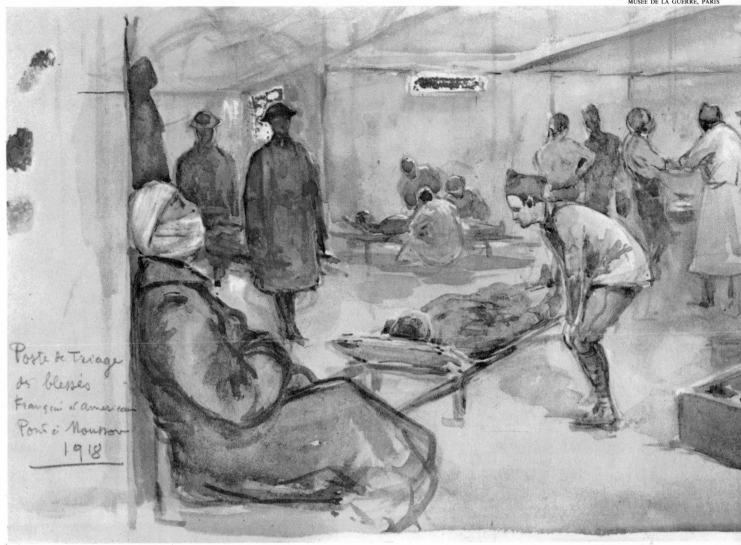

Poste de Triage
de blessés
Français et américain
Pont à Mousson
1918

into the desert. Confident that his cruel behavior would serve to protect his rear, Enver led his army into the Russian Caucasus.

Winter and the Russians devoured the Turks. Fighting in cold as low as twenty degrees below zero, floundering in snow-choked mountain passes, freezing in their light clothing, the Turks fell by thousands under the skillful and fierce onslaught of Russians who were dressed and equipped for winter combat. It was savage warfare, and death came quickly to the wounded left lying in the snow. They froze to death, as did whole battalions of soldiers caught out in the open in howling blizzards. By mid-January of 1915, Enver's force of 95,000 had dwindled to 18,000. Perhaps 30,000 men were bur-

ied or left frozen in the snow. The rest deserted, a habit with soldiers of the Ottoman Empire once they saw that their cause was lost.

Out of this northern campaign came even more intense grief for Turkey, for it made the reputation of the Russian General Nikolai Yudenich. Thereafter he was to scourge all Turkish forces from the Black Sea to the Caspian before his own crippled nation was forced to withdraw from the war. And from the defeats suffered in the cold of the Russian mountains, Turkey was to move to fresh disaster in the heat of the desert.

Turkish rule in the Middle East still included Palestine (the Holy Land) and Mesopotamia,

135

T. E. Lawrence's camel-mounted army forms a battle line.

as well as the tribes of Arabia. Here the British were to conduct two vast campaigns involving hundreds of thousands of troops in each. Here, too, the romantic figure of T. E. Lawrence was to enter history. An Englishman clad in the flowing white burnoose of the Arab, a master of guerrilla warfare, especially in such niceties as blowing up trains, Lawrence was a living legend. It was he who did so much to rally the Arabs to the Allied cause, and after the standard of Arab revolt was raised in Mecca by King Hussein, Lawrence and his hard-riding Bedouins were in the vanguard of the forces harrying the Turks.

The key to Palestine, of course, was the Gaza region. It was the gateway between Asia and Africa, between Egypt and the Holy Land. A small British army under General Sir Archibald Murray had tried to burst the Gaza gate, but had been repulsed by the Turks. In 1917, General Edmund Allenby left

France to take command in Palestine. Nicknamed "the Bull," by his soldiers, Allenby was a leader of commanding physical appearance. Soldiers were inspired by his presence. In September he started his army hammering at Gaza.

Opposing him now was General Falkenhayn, the fallen, evil genius of Verdun. He had been rushed from Germany to direct the Turkish defense. But Falkenhayn had too few troops, and Allenby was too determined to win. On November 7, the Turks abandoned Gaza. The British came in and Allenby rode onward to Jerusalem. A month later Jerusalem surrendered. The Holy City in which Christ had suffered and died was presented to Lloyd George as a Christmas present.

Thereafter, Allenby's army was invincible. He had 103,000 riflemen against 36,000 for Falkenhayn. "A tiger fighting a sick tomcat," wrote one British soldier. Perhaps, but it was a very colorful tiger.

Enigmatic Lawrence of Arabia poses in native garb above his desert camp. A night-marching camel train attached to General Allenby's army in Palestine is pictured at left.

In the first three years of its existence, the Army of the Orient never got beyond 70 miles of its headquarters in Salonika. While playing a waiting game soldiers made the best of a monotonous, disease-ridden life. In the drawing above, two soldiers use the side of a wall to write letters, while a third soldier eats soup as a child watches. At right, an Australian soldier eyes his seatmate casually picking fleas from a companion's head; the white-bearded old man at his left meditates on war and peace over his umbrella.

Algerians, Jews, Indian Moslems, Negroes from the heart of Africa, Hindus and Bedouins, all joined the British and Anzacs under Allenby's command to drive the detested Turks from the Holy Land.

In September, 1918, Allenby's army rode through the battlefield where Richard the Lion-Hearted had conquered Saladin in the Crusades. Beyond the legendary field of Armageddon (modern Megiddo), they met and destroyed two Turkish armies on the Plain of Jezreel. Then they swept into Nazareth, and by the end of the month they were driving for the city of Damascus.

Meanwhile, British arms were also triumphing in Mesopotamia.

Mesopotamia (modern Iraq) is the land that scholars often call the cradle of civilization. Its very name means "the country between the rivers": the Tigris and the Euphrates. Here, the British collided with the Turks in order to protect their Middle East oil holdings. A great army of 414,000 men under Lieutenant General Sir Stanley Maude worked its way painfully up the Tigris. In mid-March, 1917, the city of Baghdad fell to Maude's army. After Maude died of cholera (a disease afflicting the troops of both sides), Lieutenant General W. R. Marshall took command.

Marshall began driving still farther up the Tigris against the last Turkish bastion in the city of Mosul. He would reach and conquer it eventually, taking the surrender of the Turks at about the same time that the Allied army at Salonika was crushing the Bulgarians.

The Allied Army of the Orient was sent to Salonika to save Serbia. Salonika is the little Greek port city at the top of the Aegean Sea. A force moving northwest from Salonika could enter Serbia. And such a move was necessary by 1915 to

138

L'Armée de Tiers-État: Dans le Tramway à Salonique —

save that little kingdom from dire peril. After it had repulsed Austria in 1914, Serbia had been menaced by German divisions dispatched southward. Then Bulgaria, to Serbia's east, decided it was time to enter the war on the side of the Central Powers.

Aware of this, the Premier of Greece asked the Allies to help him honor his pledge to aid Serbia. By October 2, the first of the Allied troops were landing at Salonika. On October 12, two Bulgarian armies began driving west through Serbia. Then an Austro-German army of 250,000 men under the capable General August von Mackensen began plunging south. Caught between them, the Serbian Army backpedaled west all the way to the Adriatic Sea.

Now the Allies rushed more troops into Salonika. But they were too late. When they tried to march north to the rescue, the Bulgars drove them back. The Army of the Orient fell back on Salonika, where it was to remain and grow larger and larger.

By 1917 there were six hundred thousand men in the Army of the Orient. They were chiefly French and British, with some Greek, Albanian, Serbian, Italian, and Montenegrin units. Disease rather than bullets ravished this force. At last, in the fall of 1918, with both the Austro-Germans and the Turks cracking everywhere, the Army of the Orient broke through to crush the Bulgars.

Although the story of World War I has been chiefly concerned with the fighting fronts in Russia and France, the flames that licked the outer rim of the conflict were very real and very hot. Millions of men marched and suffered there. Hundreds of thousands died or were wounded. For all of them, the bullets and the shells of the outer rim were as much to be feared as those that whispered and shrieked in the bigger battles of the western front.

In 1918, these were rising to their final fury.

139

Allied resistance to the German offensives of 1918 is symbolized in Sir William Orpen's painting of a howitzer crew stripped to the waist amid the smoke of their heated weapon.

LUDENDORFF RISKS ALL

14

On January 8, 1918, Senators and Representatives of the U.S. Congress were astonished to learn that the President wished to address them all in half an hour. Many of them were not able to get to their seats before President Wilson arrived and began to deliver his famous Fourteen Points speech. Boiled down, these suggested ground rules for peace were:

1. Open covenants (international agreements without secret clauses) openly arrived at.
2. Freedom of the seas.
3. Removal of economic barriers.
4. Reduction of armaments.
5. Adjustment of colonial claims in the interest of subject peoples.
6. German evacuation of Russian territory and free determination of Russian national policy.
7. German evacuation and restoration of Belgium.
8. German evacuation of French territory; return of Alsace-Lorraine to France.
9. Readjustment of Italian frontiers on lines of nationality.
10. Peoples of Austrian Empire to be granted right of self-determination.
11. German evacuation of Rumania, Serbia, and Montenegro; and Serbia to be given access to the sea.
12. Self-determination for non-Turkish nationalities in the Ottoman Empire; the Dardanelles to be opened to ships of all nations.
13. Poland to be made independent, with access to the sea.
14. Formation of a general association of nations to keep the world peace.

The lofty ideals of the Fourteen Points provoked profound reactions among the world's leaders. Both Germany and Austria thought highly of every proposal except the ones requiring evacuation of conquered territory. Allied leaders praised the points publicly, but in private they declared that President Wilson did not understand European problems. Eventually Lloyd George and Clemenceau would meet secretly to plan how to circumvent the Fourteen Points. And to General Erich Ludendorff, the points were simply "figments of the imagination."

Ludendorff had his own plans for peace, and it was to be a peace brought about by German arms. Ludendorff was convinced that 1918 was the year of decision. Russia's departure from the war had released great bodies of troops for use in the West. Moreover, 1918 had to be the year. The effects of the British blockade were being deeply felt in Germany. Even the elite troops were making *ersatz* coffee and smoking weeds. At home, it was a lucky family indeed with enough bones to make a soup. Victory had to be now or never.

Ludendorff hoped that the new tactic of "infiltration" developed on the eastern front would carry the day. This was nothing less than Indian warfare on a grand scale. Instead of striking at strong points, German troops were taught to probe for soft spots through which they could speed to the enemy's rear. So General Ludendorff prepared his big blow. It was called Operation Michael, and it was to be followed by similar operations designed to take advantage of Michael's gains. It would fall against the British in the north.

Here, in the old battlefields of Artois and Picardy, there was very little back room for maneuver. The British almost had their backs to the Channel. If they were driven up to the water, they might be forced to evacuate. Then Ludendorff could concentrate on breaking the French Army to the south.

As soon as the weather began to thaw, the Germans got busy. Some sixty-two divisions were

In the 1915 photograph above, Kaiser Wilhelm—his withered left arm disguised by the hand-on-sword pose—inspects troops with his son, the Crown Prince (wearing a fur hat). The Kaiser hoped that plan Michael would deliver the final blow to the Allies. The painting at right shows German troops advancing through a wood in an earlier assault; their flame thrower cuts a path ahead of them. In the background French troops panic as the flames reach out for them.

brought forward. There were enough of them to place a division along every mile of front. As they moved into position, their ranks were sifted for the strongest and most warlike soldiers. These men were formed into storm groups which would make the initial assault. They would look for the weak spots, break through, and destroy the British artillery. They had rifles, pistols, light machine guns, and flame throwers. Behind them would come the regular infantry with heavier weapons. Before the attack was made, no less than six thousand guns would batter the English with shells or poison the atmosphere with gas.

As the build-up continued through March, General Sir Hubert Gough, commander of the British Fifth Army, became alarmed. He notified the High Command that the Germans were concentrating opposite him. He was able to impress General Haig,

General Ludendorff (above), nominally second in command, usurped control of the military from the weak-willed Hindenburg. By 1918, he was the virtual dictator of Germany, having gained control of the civilian population as well.

who gave him reinforcements, but the French were not impressed. General Pétain actually thought the Germans might move through neutral Switzerland to get around the Allied right flank. He was certain that if the Germans massed it was to strike the French, not the British.

Thus, on the night of March 20, the British in front of Amiens had about nineteen divisions against fifty-six German divisions. At 4:50 A.M. on March 21, the greatest artillery duel in world history began. Six thousand German guns bayed and bellowed, and twenty-five hundred British cannon thundered back. Five hours later the German storm troopers rushed forward through thick fog.

The fog served the German cause. They could get in on the Tommies without being seen. Where they broke through, they were not exposed to fire on their flanks. Sometimes the Germans stumbled off course, but generally the fog—streaked with billowing clouds of brown smoke and green gas—was the friend of the Germans.

So was their artillery. It simply smashed the British defenses and left them a smoking chaos of rubble and upturned earth. Road intersections were blanketed, artillery horse-parks, aid stations, and railheads were wiped out, and ammunition dumps were set to a monstrous crackling, like giant strings of Chinese firecrackers.

The British fought back with characteristic courage, but the Germans were unstoppable. They achieved Ludendorff's long-desired penetration the first day. This had not happened in four years of dreadful war. Victory seemed within the grasp of the Kaiser, who had come to Ludendorff's headquarters to observe the battle.

That night General Gough pulled back the Fifth Army's right wing. Next day a gap opened between his right and the left of General Byng's Sixth Army. Soon Byng had to pull back also. All of that cratered, blood-soaked ground won by the British in the dogged Somme battles of 1916 had to be surrendered. The Germans were threatening to break through into open country. Amiens might have to be abandoned to the Kaiser's onrushing troops.

General Haig appealed urgently to General Pétain to send in French reserves. But Pétain still thought that the attack in the north was merely a feint. He insisted that the true German objective was the French army in the Champagne.

Distraught, the Allies summoned a meeting of the Supreme War Council.

On March 26, even as the retreat on Amiens continued, the war chiefs of France and Britain assembled at Doullens. Their faces were gray. They seemed weary. Then General Foch spoke.

"You aren't fighting?" he rasped. "I would fight without a break! I would fight in front of Amiens. I would fight in Amiens. I would fight behind Amiens. I would fight all the time. I would never surrender!"

It was the great inspirational speech of World War I. Georges Clemenceau would use it—reworked —to electrify the French Chamber of Deputies. Three decades later Winston Churchill would use it—reworked again—to rally a weary Britain in World War II. At this moment, it inflamed the Allies. And it brought about the badly needed unity

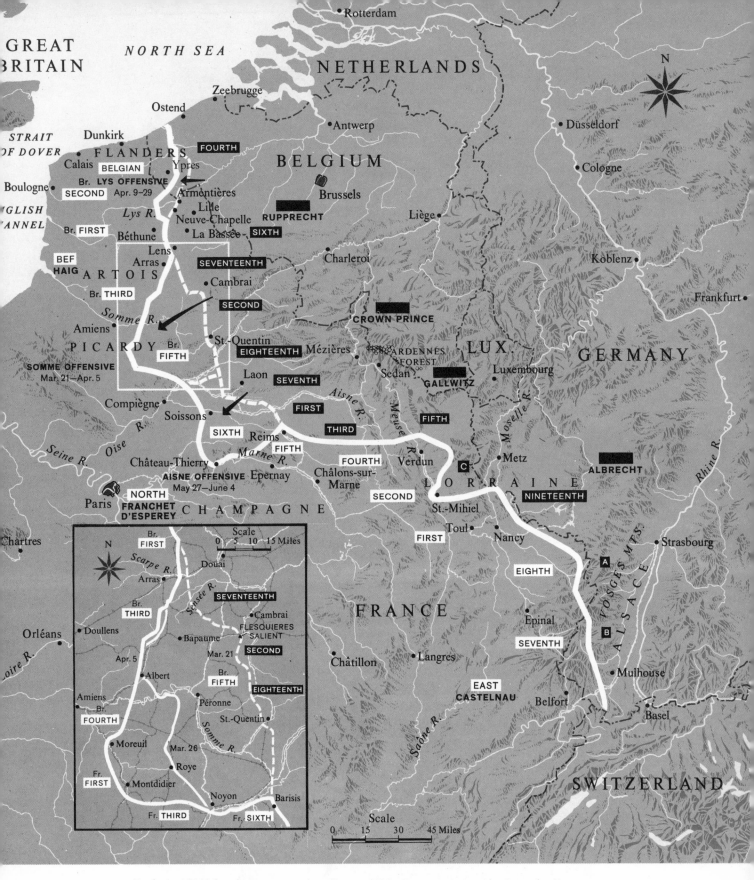

Early in 1918, by three successive offensives (black arrows)—on the Lys, the Somme, and the Aisne—Germany drove deep wedges into Allied territory. The inset shows the stages (broken white to solid white lines) of the impressive German gains on the Somme.

French troops were battered and mauled by Germany's 1918 offensives. Yet French soldiers found ways to make life at the front bearable. Canteens like the one above were built to facilitate wine distribution. And the men constructed their own snuggeries: at right, a well-entrenched cobbler makes his trade known to his comrades-in-arms.

of command. Ferdinand Foch was appointed chief of the Allied armies, and almost at once their spirits began to rise again.

On the front before Amiens, a British general named Malcolm was positively enthusiastic. To a French general who asked him how the situation was, Malcolm replied: "It is quite good, we have won the war."

General Malcolm had accurately measured the failing fighting spirit of the Germans opposite him. He appreciated what Erich Ludendorff also appreciated: that the drive on Amiens had run out of gas. On April 5, Ludendorff ended the battle.

Operation Michael had failed. It had won 1,250 square miles of desolated French countryside for the Germans, but it had also extended the German front by fifty miles. And it had not destroyed the British Army.

A week later, the driving Ludendorff hurled another thunderbolt at the old battlefield of Ypres.

German planners had called this offensive Operation George, but because it was not to be as big as planned it was renamed Georgette. The British called the fight the Battle of the Lys, after the river where the British Second and First Armies

146

line, but instead the Germans drove them out. By nightfall the Germans had pushed ahead five miles to the Lys. Farther north they drove back a weary British division. Next day the Germans scored more advances. General Haig was outwardly alarmed for one of the few times in his career. For the first time he dropped his icy manner and implored his troops to hold fast. In a famous Order of the Day issued on April 12, he said:

"There is no other course open to us but to fight it out. Every position must be held to the last man. There must be no retirement. With our backs to the wall and believing in the justice of our cause, each one of us must fight to the end."

That day, aerial attacks by the Royal Air Force hampered the German advance. On the 13th and 14th the Germans slowed down, but in the following two days they rolled forward once more. Now Haig was pleading with Foch to rush French reinforcements into the battle. Foch had already formed an Army of the North, but had not yet fed it into the line. Then, the Germans shifted farther north. They struck at the Belgian Army, which had not fought since 1914. The Belgians shattered the German attack. Now the British fell back from all the little village outposts seized in the bloody Battle of Passchendaele. But they had shortened their lines and were ready for the next German thrust.

It failed. On April 25, the Germans tried again. But by then Foch had thrown seven French divisions into the battle. At first, the French lost a vital position on the important Flanders heights screening Hazebrouck. Then they stiffened. The last German assault on the Flanders heights rolled up against them and fell back in defeat.

Once more the B.E.F. had held its ground—this time assisted by the French—the Channel ports had been saved, and the Battle of the Lys was a greater German defeat than the March failure before Amiens had been. Now, at last, General Ludendorff shifted his fire against the French in the south.

Ludendorff was still confident of final victory, and with reason. The Allies were uneasy. The political leaders distrusted the brass hats, and the military leaders disliked the "frock coats." France seethed so much internally that in March Premier

joined flanks. Actually, it was nothing less than a fourth dreadful heave over the ghastly country around Ypres.

Ludendorff struck here because it was closer to the Channel. If he could crush the B.E.F., as he still hoped, he would be much closer to the Channel ports than he was at Amiens. His general objective was the rail center of Hazebrouck, southwest of Ypres. The drive began on April 9 with another furious bombardment, and also with a slice of luck.

The Germans came straight at a tired and depressed Portuguese division in the British center. The Portuguese were to have been taken out of the

147

Clemenceau placed four valuable cavalry divisions in the interior to guard against revolt. The French Army had not yet recovered its *élan*, and the British, having taken the brunt of the German blows, were reduced to ghost divisions.

Therefore, Ludendorff was not foolish in clinging to his hopes of final victory. And he was still determined to crush the British. This third time, however, he would first prevent the French from coming to their aid. He would strike the French hard, force them to draw their reserves south, and then turn on the weakened B.E.F. again.

Ludendorff chose the Chemin des Dames sector north of the Aisne River. This had been the scene of the Nivelle Offensive in 1917. It was good country to hide troops in—no less than forty-two divisions would be employed in this "diversion"—and it was also, although Ludendorff was not aware of the fact, poorly defended (see map on page 152).

Only sixteen divisions held this sector. Five of them were battle-weary British units sent south in exchange for the fresh French ones that Foch had fed into the Lys battle. Worse, the defending troops had been placed too far forward. The ridge of the Chemin des Dames was actually suitable only as an outpost. Six to seven miles behind it was a far better ridge. Its top was broad and the ground sloped gently south so that defenders would be hidden from view. Moreover, it was between the Aisne and Vesle rivers. The Chemin des Dames was in front of both rivers. That meant that the Allied force would be fighting with two unfordable rivers at their backs.

Still, General Denis Auguste Duchêne, the commander of this force, clung stubbornly to his original dispositions.

On May 27, the German guns began thundering. The bombardment continued for four hours. Then five German divisions crashed into the Chemin des Dames. They destroyed a French division at one blow and nearly did the same to a British division on the left. They tore a gaping hole in the center of the Allied line. Nothing like that had ever happened on the western front. Delighted, the Germans surged forward. To their unspeakable joy they found the enemy in flight and the bridges over the Aisne River still standing. They began streaming over in an unchecked tide.

On the right of the collapsing Allied line the British fought desperately. On the left the French were trying to hold their ground. But in the wide-open center the Germans rolled over the French reserves who had been rushed forward to close the gap. By nightfall, the Germans had reached the Vesle River. They had worked their way past that excellent position that General Duchêne had so carelessly neglected to fortify.

Should the Germans stop? After all, the Aisne offensive was only a diversion. The true blow was to be delivered up north after enough strength had been drawn away from the B.E.F. Yes, but eighty miles away lay what city?

Paris.

Jubilant, the Germans swept forward again the next day. They gained another five miles. Miles! Fifteen miles in two days had never been heard of since trench warfare began. On and on the gray tide rolled. By June 3, the Germans were once more on the Marne River east of a place called Château-Thierry. Paris was only fifty-six miles away.

Once again the French Government prepared to flee the capital. Along the road to Paris, dusty and war-weary *poilus* mingled with crowds of terrified peasants. Farmers drove carts piled high with household goods or crates of chickens. Some had cows on the leash. Women pushed perambulators with babies in them. Sick people lay gasping on the roadside. Terror—stark and unconcealed—contorted every face.

But then, up the Paris-Metz road toward the sound of the guns, a brigade of American Marines came marching.

In the head-on combat photograph at right, German troops advance through fire and smoke past the body of a French soldier felled at the edge of a shell hole. The soldier at center gets ready to hurl a "potato-masher" grenade. During this action near the Somme, Hutier's Eighteenth Army overran Allied lines, thus achieving one objective of Ludendorff's great spring offensive. Although the German armies made extensive gains throughout the spring, these failed to bring them their much-desired final victory. Ludendorff overlooked two crucial points: inadequate German reserves to hold newly won territory; and the power of the doughboys pouring into France from the United States.

BELLEAU WOOD 15

It was not until April, 1918—a full year after America had entered the war—that U.S. troops engaged in large-scale fighting.

On that date, the 26th (Yankee) Division was attacked by the Germans at a place called Seicheprey. The Yanks lost the position, but regained it in a splendid counterattack. A month later, just below the Lys battleground, the 1st Division won a fine victory at Cantigny.

Nevertheless, the Americans had yet to be committed in a major battle, and Marshal Foch and General Pershing continued to argue over the disposition of American troops. Foch wanted to feed them piecemeal into the British and French armies, but Pershing wanted them kept in a separate U.S. Army. Then came the German breakthrough at the Chemin des Dames, and Pershing told Marshal Foch that he could have five U.S. divisions to help plug the breach.

Two of them—the 2nd and the 3rd—were rushed to the center, where the rout of the French had left a yawning gap. The 3rd moved farthest east, or to the right. They stopped the Germans at Château-Thierry. It was not, however, a big battle. Moreover, the Germans had wheeled to the west away from Château-Thierry. They were making for Belleau Wood (see overleaf).

Few places on the French map were as insignificant as Belleau Wood. It was only a hunting preserve, one mile square, in the middle of a rectangle formed by four tiny French villages. It was of use to no one. It was even north of the vital Paris-Metz

road. Yet, Belleau Wood was to become a shining name in history. Here the Americans met the Germans in their first major battle. Here the 2nd Division brought its two brigades, one of them made up of United States Marines under a tough soldier, Brigadier General James G. Harbord. Here also the German commander was to risk his offensive in a local dogfight. And here the Germans had picked on the wrong people. The Marine Brigade was unique —a little group of sea soldiers in an ocean of Army —and therefore was without doubt the most aggressive body of die-hards on the western front.

Those die-hards came up the Paris road on June 1. That night a message from General Duchêne was received by General Harbord. It said: "Have your men prepare entrenchments some hundreds of yards to rearward in case of need." Harbord passed the message along to his men with the remark: "We dig no trenches to fall back on. The Marines will hold where they stand."

With bayonets and mess gear pans the Marines dug in. All they did was to scrape shallow body-length pits in the ground. Joking, they called them their "graves." Actually, these were the first "foxholes." The Marines waited. French soldiers began to drift backward through the Americans. Some of them invited the Yanks to join the retreat. Lieutenant Colonel Fredric Wise shot back the scathing reply:

"Retreat hell, we just got here!"

Now the Germans had seized Belleau Wood. They began fortifying it. Machine gun nests went behind boulders and into thickets. Every hunting trail became a fire lane. All weapons were zeroed-in on a rippling green field of wheat between the wood and the Paris road. On the morning of June 6 one Marine battalion seized a commanding hill to the left of the wood. Another on the right made for the southern edge of the forest. And a third in the center went "through the wheat."

American troops were used to give muscle to the Allied forces around Château-Thierry. On the opposite page are two water colors made soon after that battle: the upper one is A.E.F. artist Harvey Dunn's view of a Yank street fighter; the lower shows a doughboy standing guard in Château-Thierry after the Yanks had captured the town.

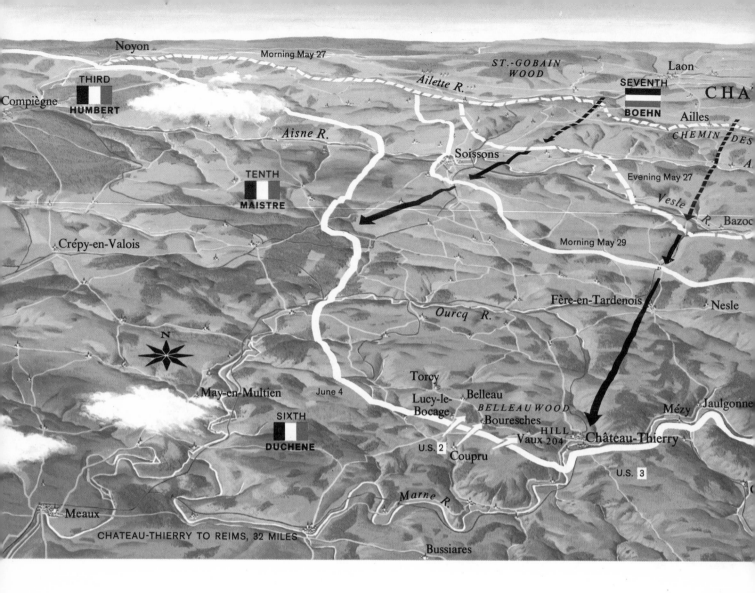

It was waving wildly, not from the wind but from the storm of German bullets sweeping through it. Americans began to fall. Grizzled old Sergeant Dan Daly swung his bayoneted rifle over his head in a forward sweep. "C'mon, you so-and-so's," he yelled to his men. "Do you want to live forever?" They leaped forward, and fell in droves. Heads down so that their helmets also covered their necks, driving into the lead storm like men battling a blizzard, they pressed stubbornly on. At the very edge of the wheat field the assault collapsed, and the Marines were pinned down.

But on the right the Marines had plunged into the forest and a terrible hand-to-hand fight began. Slithering on their bellies from rock to rock, the Americans hurled their grenades—and went leaping into machine gun nests with lunging bayonets. By nightfall, the Americans held Belleau Wood's south-

ern extremity. They also held the village of Bouresches farther right after having taken it by storm.

Still, a dreadful tree-to-tree fight was to rage for four more days in the hellish gloom of Belleau Wood. Then, on June 11, the Marines pulled back to allow Allied artillery to batter the Germans. After the barrage, the Marines drove back in to capture two thirds of the smoking, blasted forest. Once again the bullet-for-bullet battle raged. Frantic, the German commander fed more and more regiments into the wood—but the wild Americans, whom the Germans were already calling "Devil Dogs," fought on.

On June 16, exhausted, the Marines were relieved by the 7th Infantry of the 3rd Division. Twice the soldiers of the 7th charged, and twice they were beaten back.

Its ranks filled with replacements, supported by

152

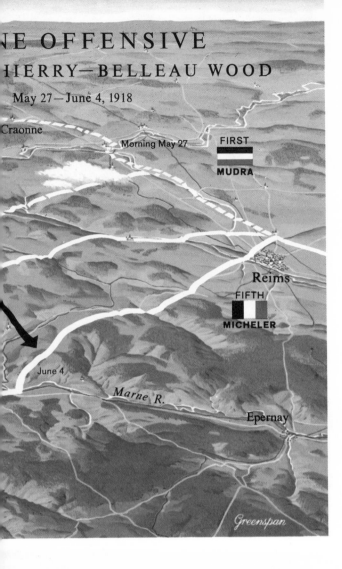

E OFFENSIVE
HIERRY—BELLEAU WOOD
May 27—June 4, 1918

Craonne

Morning May 27

FIRST

MUDRA

Reims

FIFTH

MICHELER

June 4

Marne R.

Epernay

Greenspan

two companies of Army machine gunners, the Marine Brigade went back in. On June 25, the Americans broke out of the woods into the clear. Jubilant, Major Maurice Shearer reported to General Harbord: "Wood now exclusively U.S. Marine Corps."

Belleau Wood had fallen. The Germans had been stopped. The men of the gallant Marine Brigade had used up four enemy divisions, they had saved Paris, and broken the cutting edge of General Ludendorff's most dangerous—but not his last—offensive. More, their battle cries had been heard by the dispirited French. A thrill of hope ran through the Allied armies. Weary hearts were lifted up, and the gleam of victory shone in the eye of Ferdinand Foch. And from a grateful France came this reward: "the Commanding General, Sixth Army, decrees that henceforth in all official papers Belleau Wood shall bear the name, *Bois de la Brigade de Marine.*"

The bird's-eye-view map above left, traces the progress of the third 1918 German offensive (black arrows) against the French Sixth Army at the Chemin des Dames. On May 27 the German Seventh Army under General Boehn smashed through the French lines and by evening had crossed the Aisne and Vesle rivers (lower broken white line). The French retreat, continuing until May 31, opened the road from Château-Thierry to Paris, now only 50 miles away. Advance elements of the U.S. 3rd Division met the Germans at Château-Thierry on May 31 and checked the assault. The Germans then wheeled toward Vaux and Belleau Wood, where they were stopped by the U.S. 2nd Division. Thus the German drive begun nine days before was finally halted 35 miles from its origin. Above is A.E.F. artist Wallace Morgan's sketch of a dressing station near Belleau Wood.

Men of the U.S. Marine Corps fought their way to victory and world acclaim when they drove the Germans from Belleau Wood, thereby blocking the road to Paris. Among the best pictures of leathernecks in action were those drawn by Marine Corps artist-historian Captain John W. Thomason, Jr. His sketches at the top of these pages show a detachment stepping out under the watchful eye of its leader; a marching Marine with rifle slung casually over his shoulder; a cautious attacker; and a successful capture of a German. In the battle scene above, Thomason depicts a leatherneck amid shellfire. And in the dramatic water color at left he shows one Marine fighting hand-to-hand while another bayonets a German about to fire.

In preparation for the Allied counteroffensive near Soissons, a column of French and American troops, including a horse-drawn ammunition train, heads toward the front lines.

COUNTEROFFENSIVE 16

Although the Americans had not won the war, they had forced Erich Ludendorff to revise his earlier poor estimate of them. "Personnel must be called excellent," Ludendorff wrote. "Spirit of troops is high. Moral effect of our fire does not materially check the advance of the infantry. Nerves of the Americans are still unshaken."

So also were the nerves of Erich Ludendorff. He believed that the Aisne offensive had not drawn in enough French reserves. He resolved to lure more of them into battle. Only then would he hurl "Hagen"—the code word for the northern thrust—at the British.

So a fourth German offensive was launched against the French south of the Amiens bulge. It began on June 9, and although the Germans scored a nine-mile penetration on the first day, the attack eventually faltered. It was ended after General Charles Mangin launched a spirited counterattack. Undaunted, Ludendorff ordered a fifth strike. This came on July 15 and was known as the Second Battle of the Marne, or Champagne-Marne.

In Champagne, one-armed General Henri Gouraud had prepared a "defense in depth." Line after line of prepared positions awaited the Germans. They came rolling forward into them and were torn to pieces by ferocious artillery barrages. Farther to the west, in the area around Château-Thierry, the Germans were more successful. They went streaming south of the Marne. They washed around the U.S. 38th Infantry of the 3rd Division, but they could not budge the doughboys.

"The time may come when Americans may have to give ground," Colonel Ulysses Grant McAlexander told his men. "But right now our job is so to impress Germans with our willingness to fight that their morale will be destroyed."

The 38th held, earning for itself the nickname Rock of the Marne. But if the Marne right was held firm by the U.S. 3rd Division, the left was buckling under a hurricane bombardment. Attacking under a smoke screen, the Germans drove a bridgehead four miles deep into the French line. Once again, official Paris was alarmed. Premier Clemenceau thought of relieving Marshal Foch.

But Foch was not dismayed. He had prepared his riposte. A blanket of bombs and artillery fell upon six German divisions across the Marne between Soissons and Château-Thierry. Next, a pickup French Tenth Army was formed under the fierce General Charles Mangin. Its orders were to counterattack in the Marne bulge and drive the Germans back over the river. Its spearhead was composed of the French Moroccan Division in the center, flanked left and right by the U.S. 1st and 2nd. On July 18, following a drenching cloudburst and a brief artillery barrage, the counterstroke began (map, p. 161).

Moroccans and Yanks plunged into rain-washed, ravine-split countryside. Tanks rolled ahead of them, taking the Germans by surprise. The following infantry smashed straight through the German front. Within a few hours the 2nd Division on the right had taken its first day's objective. But the Moroccans had slowed, and the 2nd's soldiers and Marines were raked from their left by Germans still secure in their positions. The Americans moved to silence the enemy fire.

On the spearhead's far left, doughboys of the 1st Division struggled through waist-deep marsh water in the face of German machine gun fire. American losses mounted, but the 1st had reached its objective line by noon.

Elated to find the German front broken so soon, General Mangin sent his reserves rushing into the battle. It went on for three days. At its close, the Germans were in full retreat—scrambling back over the Marne River.

Farther south, at Château-Thierry, counterattacking French and Americans drove the retiring Germans before them. Doughboys of the 3rd Division crossed the Marne in pursuit.

Germany's Great Retreat had begun. The days of Ludendorff's offensives were over. Operation *Hagen* was suspended and then abandoned, and from July 18 onward, the Germans were on the defensive.

All along the line came Ferdinand Foch, proposing new offensives, urging his generals on. Lifted up by the success of the Second Marne, elated to see how American dash and daring had given his dejected *poilus* back their wonderful fighting *élan*, Marshal Foch asked himself at the end of July:

"What am I risking, after all? . . . You can prepare for the worst and another year of fighting, but there is no crime in hoping for the best—decisive victory within a few months."

In such a mood, Foch at once fell in with General Haig's proposal for a massive British attack on the big German bulge at Amiens. He not only approved it, he expanded it. He added the French First and Third Armies to the British Fourth. The Fourth was truly an Allied force. The U.S. 33rd Division was attached to the British on the left, the center was held by the veteran Australian Corps, and the right by the splendid Canadian Corps. In front were massed twelve tank battalions: 324 heavies, 97 lights, and 12 armored cars.

Amiens was to be another Cambrai on a much bigger scale. Again, surprise was to be the chief element. The Fourth Army's artillery was moved to the front by night, and sixty trainloads stole into position that way. To smother the rumble of arriving tanks, the Royal Air Force unleashed a noise bar-

Artillery as well as troops played a major role in turning the German "Peace Drive" into a retreat. At right, in a painting by Rudolf Stanley-Brown, an American gun crew maneuvers a camouflaged 305-mm. gun mounted on railroad tracks for greater mobility. In the unique photograph at left, a direct hit by Allied artillery stampedes horses in a German gun unit.

rage of its own. Troops were given no information of the attack until twenty-four hours before they went "over the top." That way, any prisoners taken by the Germans during the build-up days would have no information to divulge. August 8 was the date for the attack. At midnight, a thickening ground mist blanketed the battle zone. Two hours later visibility was at zero. The troops began moving into the assembly areas, groping their way through fog. Behind them the tanks waited. Then they, too, came forward. Moving at a snail's pace, following white tapes, they crept to the fore of the infantry. All

A.E.F. artist George Harding drew doughboys charging into a German trench during the Allied drive near Verdun. In mid-air are "potato mashers" hurled at the incoming troops.

was in readiness. Masses of men and machines lay beaded with water within the glistening fog. Then, at 4:20 A.M., two thousand guns spoke with a single bellowing voice—and the British Fourth Army swept forward into battle.

Surprise was complete. Except for the left flank, where a German counterbarrage of gas shells delayed the British, no answering hail of shells fell upon these soldiers and tanks moving across no man's land. Instead, the Allied rolling barrage moved in a line of flame two hundred yards ahead of the advance. Every three minutes it lifted and advanced another hundred yards. In fifteen minutes the fatal area where so many attacks had been caught and broken had been safely passed. The Allies were into the German front lines, driving the startled enemy away in a rout.

Now, with daylight, the French armies on the right were moving into action. They had been late starting, but that had been fortunate. The Germans,

convinced that only the British were attacking, had shifted to the right—and the French went roaring through the gap. On and on the Allied tide rolled, and everywhere ahead of it roamed the rampaging tanks—spreading terror and demoralizing the Germans by the mere rumble of their approach.

Thus August 8, 1918, the day that General Ludendorff called "the black day of the German Army in the history of this war." A penetration seven miles deep had been gained. Three days later the Battle of Amiens began sputtering to its close. It had cost the Allies about 46,000 casualties, while Germany suffered an estimated 75,000 casualties, also losing 30,000 prisoners and 500 guns.

In comparison to the earlier bloodlettings of the war, Amiens might not seem a great battle. But battles are measured by their effect on a war, not by the number of men killed or maimed. Amiens, then, was the turning of the tide. It capped a series of German setbacks, beginning with the failure of

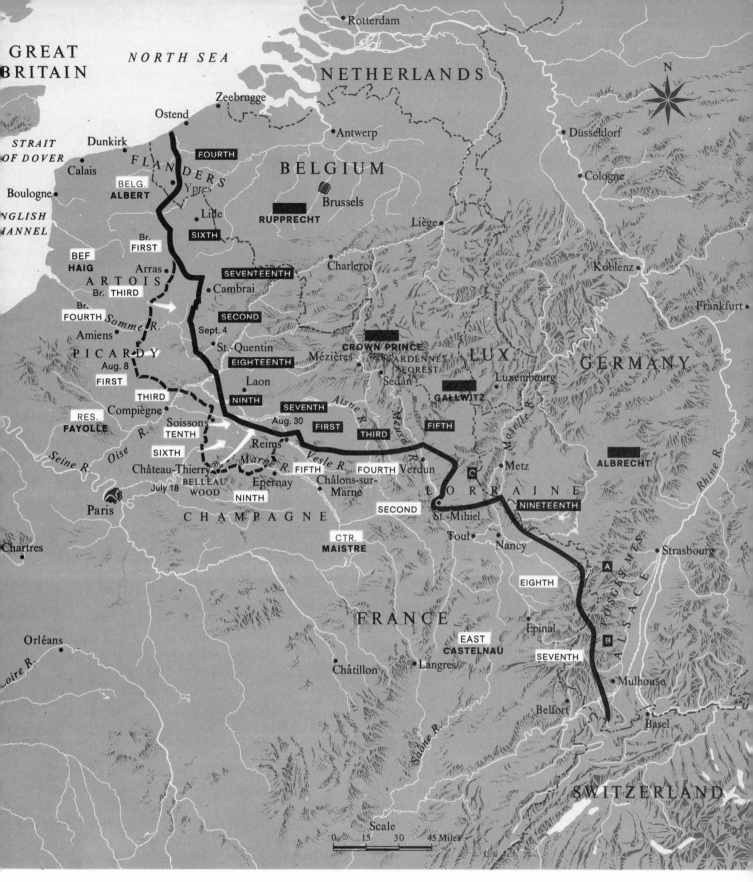

Allied counteroffensives (white arrows) during the summer of 1918 drove the Germans north from the Marne to the Vesle River and eliminated their deep salient on the Somme.

Ludendorff's offensives and stretching through Belleau Wood and the Second Marne.

After Amiens, the Germans knew that they could not win. They did not think that they would lose, but they realized that victory was beyond them.

"It is no longer possible to make the enemy sue for peace by an offensive," Ludendorff told the Kaiser on August 13. "The defensive alone cannot achieve that object. Termination of the war must be brought about by diplomacy."

It was not diplomacy, but Allied arms again, that would end it.

A wounded French soldier walks dejectedly through a bleak landscape behind the lines.

Away from the front a sol-dier's existence had the hum-drum aspect of everyday life. The painting at right shows an off-duty soldier perusing a newspaper while his com-panion appears stupefied with boredom. Above, soldiers chat and relax in a quiet sector.

VICTORY

17

Historians are generally agreed that the decisive factor in World War I was the American Army. This does not mean that the Yanks won the war. It means only that American manpower made the difference. Britain and France—and to a much lesser extent Italy—were like weary wrestlers struggling to subdue a weakening giant. At the right moment America appeared to add her weight to the struggle and bear Germany to the earth.

That weight—the American Expeditionary Forces—had reached one million men before the Battle of Amiens. After Amiens, there were a quarter of a million Yanks arriving monthly in France. Now, with the passage of the hour of crisis, General Pershing was able to form his divisions into a separate American Army. This United States First Army went into its first action in the Battle of Saint-Mihiel.

Saint-Mihiel was the last big German bulge in the Allied line. It was situated about a third of the way up the front from Switzerland. Against it, Pershing poised a force of 665,000 men, including a corps of French Colonials. They were to attack it from every side, but before they did, the largest aerial armada in history was formed to batter the bulge.

Nearly fifteen hundred planes—mostly French and British—led by the famous American commander Colonel Billy Mitchell, dropped a rain of bombs on Saint-Mihiel. Then thirty-two hundred guns began roaring at 1 A.M. of a black, drizzly September 12. Four hours later the Yanks went in.

Pershing's attack had caught the Germans on one foot. They had been preparing to depart from Saint-Mihiel just as the bombs and the shells came down. An army turned to depart is not too well prepared to fight, and the U.S. First Army swept through the blackened stumps of Saint-Mihiel to overrun the

Upon hearing the news of the armistice, American infantry-men on the western front raise their voices in a loud cheer.

German trenches in the first day. Swarms of startled men in coal-scuttle helmets came pouring out of the dugouts with their hands in the air. Some strong points resisted fiercely, of course, but within forty-eight hours of the attack the Saint-Mihiel salient had been erased (see map on page 168).

Two weeks later Pershing's doughboys were driving into the grim meat grinder of the Meuse-Argonne.

At the end of August, Marshal Ferdinand Foch had unveiled his master plan for victory with the warlike cry: "Everyone to the battle!" Come fall everyone—British, French, Belgians, and Americans—was to attack the Germans along a massive front from Verdun to the North Sea. For the Americans, Foch had selected possibly the grimmest fighting country on the western front.

Roughly, this was the terrain lying between the Meuse River on the right and the Argonne Forest on the left. The Germans had turned this sector into a wicked labyrinth of barbed wire, steel, and concrete. The Meuse-Argonne—a jumble of hills and smaller ridges reaching out from a formidable hogback ridge—was made for defense. Because the hogback split the front, it canalized the attack along both its sides. Thus, the Germans knew where to expect assault and they had concentrated their positions and troops in the right places. Even the 8 to 1 superiority in numbers worked against the Americans. They presented far too many aboveground targets to their enemies, who stayed safely underground and were prepared to sell their lives dearly.

On September 26, following the usual rolling barrage augmented by an aerial strike from 800 planes, the doughboys jumped off. At first the going was good. Then the effects of the bombardment wore off and the Germans struck back. Next, the jumbled terrain served to disorganize the attackers. By nightfall of the second day, the Meuse-Argonne push became bogged down in confusion. The U.S. First

Army paused, and as it did, the Germans rushed in reinforcements.

Thereafter the Meuse-Argonne became one of those savage shot-for-shot slugging matches made more miserable by the autumnal rains and the raw cold of approaching winter. Gradually, even the rocklike Black Jack Pershing lost some of his assurance, finally turning over command of the First Army to Major General Hunter Liggett so as to free himself for the affairs of the A.E.F. alone.

General Liggett was a capable commander. He was far overweight, but he made light of that condition with the remark: "Fat's all right provided it's not from the neck up." Under Liggett the Meuse-Argonne drive picked up. It was still a stubborn, step-by-step advance, but the American attack had more snap and precision. Meanwhile, General Pershing formed the U.S. Second Army under General Robert Lee Bullard, the bluff and bold soldier who had led the 1st Division and who was a favorite with the men. Although the Americans eventually drove to victory in the Meuse-Argonne, more spectacular Allied gains were being made on the left.

On September 28, the Belgians, British, and French on the extreme left slogged forward in a torrent of rain. By the next day, however, the British

had recovered Passchendaele Ridge and the drive was gaining momentum.

Below them, three British armies went smashing ahead, sustained hard losses, but continued fighting on until they had crashed through the Hindenburg Line by October 6.

In the Champagne, still farther south, General Gouraud's French Fourth Army forced the Germans to withdraw after the invincible U.S. 2nd Division captured Mont Blanc Ridge in a fierce fight.

All along Foch's massive front, now, the Germans were being forced to retreat. Worse for the Kaiser, at about this time General Allenby had van-

quished the Turks in Palestine and General Franchet d'Esperey's Army of the Orient had broken out of Salonika and begun the destruction of the Bulgars.

Everywhere General Erich Ludendorff looked he saw disaster or defeat. At his headquarters in Spa on the evening of September 28, Ludendorff appeared before his staff to review the situation. The *de facto* chief of the German armies began to justify his own actions. Then he began raging against everyone in general. He accused his own officers of disloyalty, charged the Imperial Navy with treachery, called the German people a pack of cowards, and sneered at the Kaiser as a weakling. Luden-

An American convoy (left) moves toward the front lines. Above, a busy U.S. gun crew builds up a pile of shell casings thrown off by their 75-mm. gun.

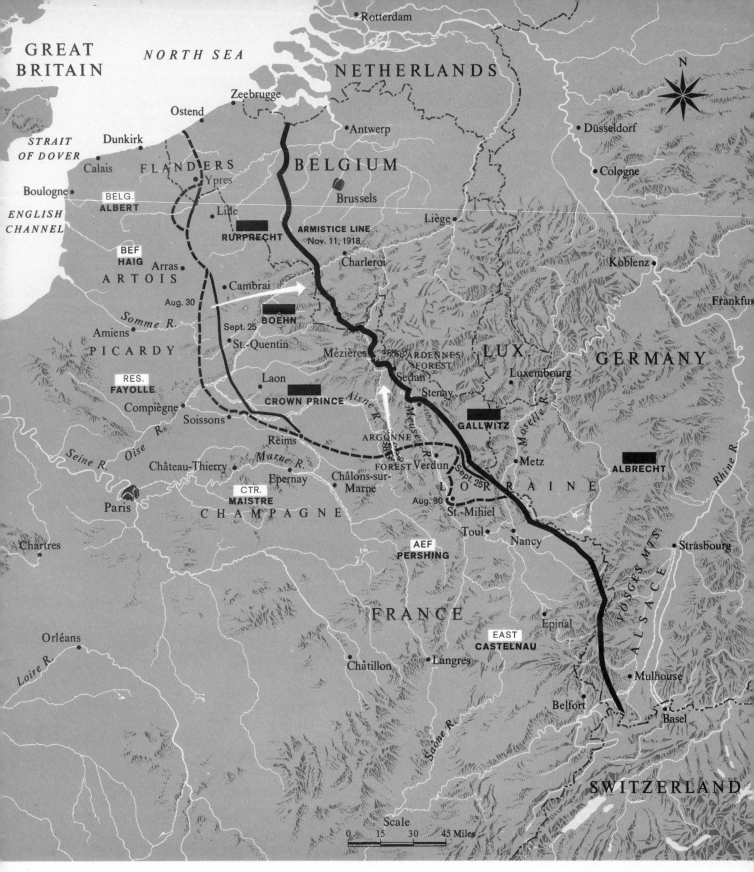

The Allied advance (white arrows) from September to November, 1918, culminated in an
"Everyone to the battle" victory drive that pushed Germany back to the armistice line.

dorff's face grew purple. His veins began to stand out like ropes on his neck and forehead. His words became blurred. Then, foaming at the mouth, he swayed and sank to the floor in a convulsive fit.

Later that night, still trembling, Ludendorff called on Hindenburg and advised him that all was lost. Germany must return all conquered territory to the Western powers and try to negotiate a peace based on the famous Fourteen Points of President Wilson. Next day the Kaiser and other high German officials arrived in Spa. The Kaiser was also trembling. Only recently his cousin, Czar Nicholas II, together with his wife and children had been killed by the Communists. Kaiser Wilhelm feared the same treatment from German revolutionaries. Already a group known as the Spartacists was calling upon the people to overturn the state. A Socialist newspaper had openly declared: "Germany, we are resolved, will haul down her flag for all time, without having brought it home victorious." Finally, the noose draped around the neck of the German economy by the British blockade was being drawn tighter and tighter, and even the loyalty of the troops was faltering. Fresh troops arriving at the front were taunted by war-weary veterans, who cried: "Blacklegs, you are prolonging the war!"

Kaiser Wilhelm was all for peace, now, and he summoned Prince Max of Baden to the post of Chancellor and the task of peacemaking. Max did not answer the summons until October 4, the day the western front erupted in flames again. Then he delayed another twenty-four hours before cabling President Wilson.

"To avoid further bloodshed," Prince Max declared, "the German Government requests the President to arrange the immediate conclusion of an armistice on land, by sea and in the air."

More delays followed, and still men were dying. President Wilson, keeping the German offer a secret from his Allies, asked Prince Max if he accepted the Fourteen Points. After this, on October 6, the suspicious Clemenceau and Lloyd George held a secret meeting. On the next day, certain people who were still fighting the war took events out of the hands of those who were trying to end it.

On October 8, an American platoon in the Argonne rounded up a group of surrendered Germans —only to be cut down themselves by more Germans farther away. At this moment, Corporal Alvin York shot down the German machine gunners with his rifle. More Germans charged and York picked them off, one by one. Then, seizing a pistol, York rounded up the remaining enemy in the sector and herded them back as prisoners.

It was an outstanding feat of arms, and it not only made York the most famous doughboy of World War I, it also made public the treachery of the Germans who had lured the American platoon to disaster by the pretense of surrender. Two days later one German submarine sank a passenger vessel with the loss of 300 lives, while another sent the

Corporal Alvin C. York poses near the spot where in 1918 he captured a German platoon and seized 132 prisoners.

mail boat *Leinster* to the bottom with 520 passengers. The Allied world trembled with rage, and President Wilson cut off the correspondence with Prince Max by informing him that the Allies could never deal with such an enemy. The Allies would set the terms of the armistice, Wilson said, and there would be no give-and-take discussions.

Prince Max tried to appease the President, but Wilson would not be budged from his position. Now the other Allied leaders learned of the correspondence, and they firmly backed Wilson—although they would not soon forget that the Presi-

dent had ignored their opinions in the beginning.

Meanwhile, the Allied armies were forcing Germany's answer. They were breaking through. On October 23, President Wilson indicated to Prince Max that he might talk with him if such German leaders as Ludendorff were expelled from power. Max immediately told the Kaiser that unless Ludendorff was dismissed, he would resign.

The Kaiser agreed, and Erich Ludendorff set aside his swagger stick, put on dark glasses and a false beard, and fled for neutral Sweden. Then on October 30, Turkey capitulated. Four days later the

Stunned doughboys, survivors of the bloody Meuse-Argonne offensive, guard German prisoners carrying a stretcher. The Meuse-Argonne was expected to bring another swift victory to the Allies but instead dragged on for over six weeks, claiming 117,000 American casualties. Despite the heavy toll, General Pershing counted the battle as a Yankee victory.

British broke through the Germans in Belgium and began attacking their rear. General Wilhelm Groener, Ludendorff's replacement, went to the front and saw the ruin of the German dream. Rushing back to Spa, he told Hindenburg: "We shall have to cross the lines with a white flag. Even a week will be too long. Do it Saturday [November 9]."

Now the sailors of Germany took a hand in the plot. Admiral Scheer had ordered the High Seas Fleet out of port. He intended to give battle and to go down with colors flying. But his sailors mutinied. They killed some of their officers and steamed back to port flying the red flags of revolution.

By November 7, all Germany was on the verge of revolution. In Berlin the Socialists were about to take to the streets in union with the Spartacists. In France that day, Marshal Ferdinand Foch sat in a railway car drawn up on a siding in Compiègne forest. He faced the trembling members of the German Armistice Commission.

"What is your purpose?" Foch snapped to the leader, Matthias Erzberger. "What do you want of me?"

Erzberger murmured that he had come to hear the armistice "proposals" of the Allies.

"I have no proposals to make," Foch grunted, and the Germans saw at once that they could not ask for terms. They must accept whatever conditions were laid down. Terms were read out, and Erzberger and his commissioners learned that the Allies desired the end of Germany as a military power.

Erzberger asked for an immediate cease-fire. It was refused. For some romantic reason the Allies wished the war to end on the eleventh hour of the eleventh day of the eleventh month. Until then, more men would die. Informed of the delay, Kaiser Wilhelm told General Groener:

"I will wait here in Spa for the armistice, and then return home at the head of my army."

"Sire, you no longer have an army," Groener replied. "The army will march home in peace. But it no longer stands behind Your Majesty."

Wilhelm turned white. He lashed out at Groener in a tirade. Next day, however, as Groener returned with Hindenburg, the Kaiser snapped, "You no longer have a War Lord," and refused to speak to him further.

Hindenburg then took over the conversation: "I

must advise Your Majesty to abdicate and to proceed to Holland," he said, and the Kaiser bowed to that counsel.

Before daylight on November 10, the cream-and-gold imperial train rolled north from Spa. Within it, in crushed silence, sat Wilhelm. At the border he changed to a private car that took him to the château of his friend, Count Godard Bentinck. Not until after the car had clattered over the drawbridge to the estate did the Kaiser speak. "And now," he told the count, "I must have a cup of good, hot, strong English tea. Yes, make it English."

Thus the last of the German emperors passed from the pages of history. On the following day, November 11, 1918, an eerie silence came over the western front.

One by one the guns fell silent. Here and there came the clattering of a machine gun being emptied into the air. On the eleventh hour all was still. Like moles, the men came up into the weak and winter sunlight. They looked at each other, dumfounded. Then they began to laugh, they began to cry, they began to shout and cheer, to pound each other on the back—and to walk slowly, hesitantly, but nevertheless erect, onto those no man's lands of shell-pocked mud that symbolized this dreadful war that was now ending.

No bullets whispered, no shells whined, and they went forward to greet "the Krauts," to smoke and trade and to come back with fewer cigarettes but laden with Iron Crosses and Lugers. That afternoon, like joyful children released from school, they played hopscotch, duck-on-the-rock, and blindman's buff. That night they shot off Very lights and colored rockets.

They sat there watching, these men of both sides, while a great peace came upon them and a sickle moon shone faintly over all that tortured earth.

The two waiting trains photographed at left were the scene of the armistice signing in the Compiègne forest. Foch's train is on the side track at left. After his abdication, Wilhelm II sought political asylum in neutral Holland. The former Kaiser is shown at right (wearing a cape over his shoulders) strolling with a companion through the garden of his refuge in the Netherlands.

THE PEACE

18

Combat had ceased in World War I, but the specters who are identified in the Bible as the Four Horsemen of the Apocalypse—Famine, Disease, Destruction, and Death—continued their devastating ride across the world.

There was death because civil wars continued to ravage Russia, and because Greece, scavenger hunting in the ruins of the Ottoman Empire, warred with the Turks for two years. In September, 1922, Kemal Atatürk, or Mustafa Kemal, one of the heroes of Gallipoli, crushed the Greeks at Smyrna and began to build modern Turkey.

There was destruction because the red tide of Communism had already begun to sweep westward out of Russia. It threatened to destroy democracy in Germany and flourished for a brief period in Hungary. It might have overrun all of Western Europe had not a valiant Polish army under the command of Marshal Józef Pilsudski conquered it at the gates of Warsaw in 1920.

There was disease because of the widespread devastation that had ravaged the Continent. The great influenza epidemic of 1918–19 killed millions of persons and took the lives of five hundred thousand Americans, at home or in the frozen mud encampments of France. Typhus, smallpox, and other plagues stalked the ruins of cities and countrysides.

There was famine, in Germany most of all because the Allies unwisely and inhumanely continued the blockade, and in the rest of the war-torn world because damage and neglect had shattered the economies of all participants except the United States. During this time an American engineer named Herbert Hoover became world-famous for organizing famine relief for Belgium, Russia, and other starving nations.

Much of this travail had been caused by the war itself, but much of it was also due to the delay in arranging for peace treaties between the victors and the vanquished.

The peace conference did not begin until January, 1919, chiefly because Prime Minister Lloyd George, eager to exploit British gratitude for victory, called the general election that returned him to office. Then he joined Premiers Clemenceau and Orlando of France and Italy and President Wilson at Versailles. This was the very place in which France had accepted humiliating terms from Germany in 1871, and the selection of it indicated that France was out for vengeance.

It was difficult to blame her. Twice within the memory of middle-aged men the Germans had hurled themselves upon the French. Premier Clemenceau was determined that there should be no third time. Moreover, his thirst for revenge was sharpened by the vandalism of General Ludendorff, who had ordered French coal mines wrecked before the German retreat began. Clemenceau was determined to make Germany pay for this. With Lloyd George and Orlando he was convinced that Germany must be stripped of all military power and held down economically so that the battered Allies might get a head start in the postwar race for recovery.

President Wilson opposed this scheme. He might actually have defeated Lloyd George, Clemenceau, and Orlando combined, for he came to the peace conference the hero of all Europe, a man whose international prestige and popularity eclipsed that of all other peace delegates. But Mr. Wilson frittered this advantage away and hardened the other Allied ministers in their opposition to him. He had already done the same to the Republican opposition at home by passing over the G.O.P. leaders in com-

A painting by Sir William Orpen re-creates the signing of the peace treaty at Versailles. A German delegate (seated foreground) starts to sign the document as Clemenceau (center), Wilson (left), and Lloyd George (right) look on.

posing his official peace party. He went on to anger the doughboys by tying up the big liner *George Washington* for his personal use when it might have been employed in ferrying doughboys home. Nor would Wilson accept Clemenceau's invitation to visit the French industrial regions that Germany had deliberately wrecked to cripple a trade rival. Finally, President Wilson regarded his Fourteen Points—especially the formation of the League of Nations—as a sacred crusade, and he was inclined to resist any attempt to conclude a peace on any other basis.

Thus, the peace conference became a wrangle between Wilson and the other three ministers. Italy, France, and Britain—bound by secret treaties—lost all judgment and turned the conference into a scramble for spoils. Instead of trying to patch up the tattered world, they cut it up all over again. Wilson fought them, and eventually he and Clemenceau refused to talk to each other. During one argument, Clemenceau insinuated that Lloyd George was a liar, and the British chieftain jumped up, grabbed him by the collar, and demanded an apology. President Wilson had to break them apart. Then Italy, miffed by Wilson's attempt to balk her desire to feed on Austrian lands, withdrew for a time.

Meanwhile, not one of the defeated powers was allowed to attend the conference, a practice unheard of in European affairs. Moreover, the smaller nations were placed on the sidelines as spectators, in spite of Allied declarations that the war had been fought to uphold the rights of small powers.

Eventually, the treaties were worked out. Turkey was finished as an empire, clinging only to her European toe hold at Constantinople (Istanbul) and to the peninsula of Asia Minor. France and England divided up Turkey's lost territories under League of Nations "mandates," or orders. The Austrian Empire, or Austria-Hungary, was also dismantled. The new nations of Yugoslavia and Czechoslovakia were formed out of former Austrian provinces; Austria became a tiny state without ports and fettered by a weak economy; and Hungary fared only slightly better. Germany's overseas empire was also distributed under League of Nations mandates, with Japan profiting most in the Pacific. Poland, which had passed out of existence in 1795, was brought back

into being and enlarged with lands from Germany.

These new states were to act as "buffers" hemming in both Germany and Austria, while to the west France regained Alsace-Lorraine and the Allies occupied all German land west of the Rhine. East of the Rhine the Allies planned to establish a "demilitarized" zone thirty miles deep. All German rivers were to be thrown open to the world's commerce, the Kiel Canal between the North Sea and the Baltic would be internationalized, and Germany was to acknowledge her sole responsibility for World War I. Finally, a war-damages bill of $32 billion was to be paid the Allies.

In the spring of 1919, a German delegation came to Versailles and listened aghast to the terms. A furious delegate said to Clemenceau, "What will history say of this?" The Tiger of France snapped back: "It will not say that Belgium invaded Germany!"

Nevertheless, that vengeful spirit was not going to help bring peace to the world. When Herbert Hoover heard of the terms he became so distressed that he left his bed to walk the streets of Paris. He realized that Germany—the chief producer of Europe—was likely to be strangled by such exactions. On the one hand she was to be impoverished, on the other forced to pay a huge war bill. Germany could not possibly overcome such a handicap, Hoover and other foresighted men reasoned, and the results to Europe and the United States were bound to be very grave indeed.

Gradually, Lloyd George came to see the folly of such a harsh peace, but he could not dissuade his colleagues. Much as the German people protested, the treaty had to be signed. Germany had no army to resume the war, and the blockade would not be lifted until she signed.

This she did, on June 28, 1919, amid great pomp and pageantry in that very glittering Hall of Mirrors at Versailles in which the German Empire had been proclaimed at the expense of France. Germany's defeated allies signed later on.

Thus, World War I came to an end. Its cost in blood and treasure had been hideous. Casualties, of course, are by their nature almost impossible to measure. Some estimates of the loss in human lives, however, put the figure at thirteen million dead soldiers and thirteen million dead civilians. In addi-

CONTINUED ON PAGE 180

At left, Clemenceau, Wilson, Lloyd George, and Orlando (left to right) work out the terms of the peace treaty. The Versailles settlement considerably changed the map of Europe (see prewar map, page 12): nine new nations emerged (shaded areas). The Austrian Empire was carved into Austria, Hungary, Czechoslovakia, and Yugoslavia (incorporating Montenegro and innocent Serbia). Much disputed Alsace-Lorraine was returned to France.

A commemorative victory parade under the Arc de Triomphe (left) was the first of many festive reviews for the victorious Yanks. Similar scenes occurred throughout the United States as whole units began to return home. The home-coming celebrations were topped by a huge victory parade up New York City's Fifth Avenue on September 10, 1919. But the soldiers had learned that war was not a pageant of bands and banners.

179

tion, there were twenty million wounded soldiers, three million prisoners, nine million war orphans, five million war widows, and ten million war refugees. The dead numbered twice as many as in all major wars fought between 1790 and 1913. And the cost has been estimated at $332 billion. If translated into the terms of today's inflated dollar, that astronomical figure might be tripled.

All this agony and ordeal—this Famine, Disease, Destruction, and Death—had it been worth it? Had it brought the world a stable peace? Had it made the world safe for democracy?

For a while it did. But the collapse of the empires only created a vacuum into which new empires—such as Japan and Italy—and new movements—such as Communism and Fascism—were to rush. The Treaty of Versailles did not guarantee peace and stability. Its inevitable effects were described by a wise American soldier, General Tasker H. Bliss, who said: "We are in for a high period, followed by a low period. Then there will be the devil to pay all around the world."

The postwar "boom" of the twenties was the "high period," the Great Depression was the low, and the "devil" was even then walking ghostlike and hungry through the bleak barren streets of Munich. He was, in his own words, a "humannothing." He had been a corporal in the German Army. He had been very courageous and won medals. He had been gassed and had lain half-blind in a hospital cursing the "cowards" whom he accused of "betraying" Germany. Now, in that fateful summer of 1919, he was nearly hysterical with rage and shame to hear of "the great betrayal," the Treaty of Versailles. Soon he and six other men would form the National Socialist German Workers Party and dedicate it to the creation of a new Germany greater and more ambitious even than the fallen Germany of the Kaiser.

The popular name of this new party was Nazi, and the name of the man was Adolf Hitler.

Out of the rubble of World War I arose a new danger to the Allies—Hitler (first row on dais, sixth from left).

CHRONOLOGY

For five years—from Sarajevo to Versailles—the explosions of World War I burst forth on nearly every part of the earth's surface. The chronology that follows is an organization of those events in terms of time, just as the word and picture narrative on the preceding pages is an organization of the war in terms of men and events.

1914

JUNE 1914

28 Archduke Francis Ferdinand of Austria-Hungary is assassinated in Sarajevo by a Serb.

JULY 1914

23 Serbia is given a 48-hour ultimatum by Austria-Hungary.

25 Serbia's conciliatory reply is rejected; Austria-Hungary calls for partial mobilization.

28 Austria-Hungary and Serbia are at war.

29 Russia begins mobilization.

AUGUST 1914

1 Germany mobilizes and declares war against Russia.

3 Germany declares war against France.

4 Great Britain declares war against Germany; Germany declares war against and invades Belgium.

7 British troops begin to arrive in France. France invades Alsace.

18 Russia invades Galicia.

22 French forces are defeated at Charleroi.

23 The Battle of Mons forces a general Allied retreat.

23 Hindenburg and Ludendorff take command of German forces in East Prussia.

26 The Battle of Tannenberg begins.

26 The British are driven back at the Battle of Le Cateau.

31 French forces fall back to the Aisne-Reims-Verdun line.

SEPTEMBER 1914

2 The Germans reach the Marne.

5 The Battle of the Marne begins.

9 The Battle of the Marne ends in a German retreat.

10 The Germans drive Russian First Army into Poland, beginning a three-day battle around Masurian Lakes.

OCTOBER 1914

9 The Germans take Antwerp.

12 The First Battle of Ypres begins.

16 The Race to the Sea ends. The battle line in the West is stabilized.

NOVEMBER 1914

2 Russia declares war against Turkey.

7 British forces land in Mesopotamia.

DECEMBER 1914

8 A German naval squadron is destroyed off the Falkland Islands.

15 After three attempts at invasion Austria is driven from Serbia.

18 The British proclaim a protectorate over Egypt.

1915

JANUARY 1915

8 A French drive is repulsed in the Battle of Soissons.

FEBRUARY 1915

4 The Germans declare the waters around Great Britain a war zone.

19 The British begin a naval attack to force the Dardanelles.

MARCH 1915

10 A limited success is achieved by the British in the Battle of Neuve-Chapelle.

18 The British naval attack on the Dardanelles fails.

APRIL 1915

22 The Germans introduce poison gas in the Second Battle of Ypres.

25 British troops land on the Gallipoli Peninsula.

MAY 1915

2 The first of two Austro-German offensives in Galicia begins.

7 The *Lusitania* is sunk.

9 The Second Battle of Artois begins.

23 Italy enters the war on the side of the Allies.

JUNE 1915

20 The German offensive in the Argonne begins.

23 The Italians launch the First Battle of the Isonzo. (It failed, as would all eleven similar offensives against the Austrians.)

JULY 1915

9 German Southwest Africa surrenders to British forces.

12 In the Dardanelles, the British make a third attack on Cape Helles, with little gain.

AUGUST 1915

4–5 The Germans enter Warsaw; the Russian retreat continues.

6 A general British attack on the Dardanelles is pinned down and finally fails (August 21).

SEPTEMBER 1915

25 The Allies begin offensives at Loos and in the Champagne.

30 The great Russian withdrawal from Poland ends.

OCTOBER 1915

14 Bulgaria joins the Central Powers to aid in defeating Serbia.

1916

FEBRUARY 1916

21 The Battle of Verdun begins, to last intermittently through June and on again into December.

MAY 1916

4 Germany briefly suspends operations against merchant shipping.

31 The Battle of Jutland.

JULY 1916

1 The Battle of the Somme begins and lasts into November.

AUGUST 1916

29 Hindenburg and Ludendorff take command of the German Army.

SEPTEMBER 1916

10 In Salonika an Allied offensive begins.

15 The British introduce tanks in the Battle of the Somme.

NOVEMBER 1916

10 The Germans invade Rumania.

18 The Battle of the Somme ends.

DECEMBER 1916

1 A Rumanian counterattack against the Germans fails.

12 Nivelle succeeds Joffre as commander of the French Army.

18 The Battle of Verdun ends after the French make gains.

19 Haig replaces French as commander of the B.E.F.

1917

JANUARY 1917

7 The Germans suspend operations against Rumania.

21 Germany announces resumption of unrestricted naval warfare.

MARCH 1917

15 The Russian revolt forces the abdication of the Czar.

APRIL 1917

6 The U.S. declares war against Germany.

16 As a result of the failure of the Nivelle Offensive, French troops mutiny. Pétain replaces Nivelle in May.

JULY 1917

1 The Russians' Brusilov Offensive makes momentary gains in Galicia.

25 The first American troops arrive in France.

31 The Third Battle of Ypres begins, lasting until November 6.

OCTOBER 1917

24 The Battle of Caporetto opens; the Italians are routed.

NOVEMBER 1917

6 The Bolsheviks take over the Russian Government.

9 The Allies form the Supreme War Council.

DECEMBER 1917

1 The Allies occupy all of German East Africa.

2 Russia withdraws from the war.

9 The British capture Jerusalem.

1918

JANUARY 1918

8 President Wilson presents his Fourteen Points.

MARCH 1918

21 The Germans begin the Somme offensive.

APRIL 1918

4 The Germans' offensive at the Somme runs down after a 30-mile gain.

9 The German offensive at Lys begins and gains 10 miles.

14 Foch is appointed Supreme Allied Commander.

MAY 1918

27 The Aisne offensive, the third German drive, breaks through to the Marne.

28 The Americans stage their first independent action in the Battle of Cantigny.

JUNE 1918

2 The French hold at the Marne; the Americans stop the Germans at Château-Thierry.

15 The Austrians are beaten back by the Italians in the Battle of Piave.

JULY 1918

15 The last German offensive, the Second Battle of the Marne, is stopped by the French.

18 The Allies push their Aisne-Marne offensive against the Germans in the Marne salient.

27 The Germans pull out of the Marne salient.

SEPTEMBER 1918

12 The Americans defeat the Germans at Saint-Mihiel.

19 A combined force of French, British, and Serbs put the Bulgarians to flight.

26 The final Allied offensive opens.

27 In the Second Battle of Cambrai, the British pierce the Hindenburg Line.

29 The Bulgarians sign an armistice.

OCTOBER 1918

14 The Allies start an offensive in Flanders.

24 The Battle of Vittorio Veneto begins (ends November 4), in which the Austrians are shattered.

27 Ludendorff resigns.

30 An armistice is signed between the British and the Turks.

NOVEMBER 1918

3 An armistice is achieved on the Italian front.

3 German sailors mutiny.

3 Americans and French clear the Argonne Forest.

6 The Germans withdraw in a general retreat.

11 At Compiègne the Germans sign the armistice prepared by the Allies.

18 The Belgians re-enter Brussels.

21 The German High Seas Fleet surrenders to British.

1919

JANUARY 1919

18 The peace conference opens in Paris.

JUNE 1919

28 Treaty of Versailles.

INDEX

Bold face page numbers indicate illustrations